The Community and Message of Isaiah 56-66

The
Community
and
Message of
Isaiah 56-66

A Theological
Commentary

Elizabeth Achtemeier

AUGSBURG Publishing House • Minneapolis

THE COMMUNITY AND MESSAGE OF ISAIAH 56-66

MANUFACTURED IN THE UNITED STATES OF AMERICA

To Marie,
upon her graduation.

*Many daughters have done excellently,
but you surpass them all.*
—Prov. 31:29

Contents

Introduction 9

Why Read the Prophets? 9

The Authors and Date of Trito-Isaiah 11

The Community Behind Trito-Isaiah 17

Some Thoughts on Studying Trito-Isaiah 26

Unfolding the Message

Part 1—Isaiah 56-59 29

Isaiah 56:1-8 31

Isaiah 56:9-12 37

Isaiah 57:1-13 40

Isaiah 57:14-21 46

Isaiah 58:1-14 50

Isaiah 59:1-20 61

Isaiah 59:21 72

Part II—Isaiah 60-62 75

Isaiah 60:1-22 77

Isaiah 61:1-11 86

Isaiah 62:1-9 94

Isaiah 62:10-12 100

Part III—Isaiah 63-66 103

    Isaiah 63:1-6 105

    Isaiah 63:7—64:12 109

    Isaiah 65:1-7 121

    Isaiah 65:8-25 126

    Isaiah 66:1-2, 3-4, 5-6, 7-9, 10-13, 14-18a 135

    Isaiah 66:18b-21 146

    Isaiah 66:22-4 149

Trito-Isaiah and the Problem of the Canon 153

Bibliography 159

Introduction

Why Read the Prophets?

The Word of God, spoken through the prophets of Israel, was intended for very specific times and situations. It was spoken into the communities of an ancient people who inhabited the Palestinian landbridge between Asia and Egypt during the first millenium B.C. The Word revealed where and how God was at work in that people's life. It assessed that people's past in the light of God's character and purpose, and it promised—indeed, it began —a future action of God toward that particular, covenant people.

There is therefore no legitimate way in which the prophetic writings can be read today as timeless truths. We may think to lift out one or another prophetic saying as a statement of an eternally valid religious or ethical principle, applicable always to the nature of God or to the character of human life; but by divesting the prophetic oracle of its concrete historical context, we turn it into a bloodless corpse, having no relation to actual human life. Through the prophets, God dealt with the realities of Israel's day-to-day living. The prophetic writings can only properly be understood in that realistic context.

Why, then, should we read the prophets? If their words apply to and influence only the past, why bother with them in the present? We are centuries removed from an Israel in exile, a Jerusalem destroyed by Babylonian troops, a defeated and impoverished population who worshiped at a ruined altar. What do those circumstances, and the Word addressed to them, have to do with us? Sufficient unto our day are our evil and problems, without bothering with those of antiquity. We live in a different world, which Trito-Isaiah and all the other prophets would not even have understood.

One fact gives us pause before we discard the prophetic writings as outdated however: Trito-Isaiah and the others who preceded and followed him spoke the Word of the living God. Having stood in the council of the Lord to perceive and to hear his deliberations (cf. Jer. 23:18; Isa. 6:1-12; 40:1-8), they were sent then to announce to their people those decisions of the God in charge of history. God's Word was put in their mouths (cf. Jer. 1:9; Ezek. 3:3) and written on their hearts (cf. Jer. 31:33; 4:19), or as in the case of Trito-Isaiah, poured into their persons by the Spirit (61:1)—messages not of their own desire and making (cf. Isa. 6:9-11; 55:8; Jer. 20:9), but from him with whom dwelt the Word (cf. Gen. 1; John 1:1-2). The prophetic sayings revealed the actions and plans and character of that Person of absolute power who rules all natural processes and all human destinies. And it just may be that what he desired and how he acted then, say in the sixth century B.C., may be analogous to what he desires and is doing now. If so, we ignore the prophetic revelation at our peril. God's Word revealed reality then; we may be required in the twentieth century to conform our lives to similar divine actions and desires.

Further, the Word which God spoke through Trito-Isaiah in the sixth century B.C., illumined God's purposes within an ongoing plan for his world. It was not a static truth, but the revelation of a divine activity which began at the creation and which now continues toward the end of history and the coming of the kingdom of God. God is on the move toward a goal. The plan goes on (cf. 1 Cor. 2:6-10). If we would have any hope, any wisdom, any proper adjustment to the real thrusts forward of nature and history, we therefore need to know all we can about the plan. God spoke his Word forward toward the future in Trito-Isaiah. What happened to that Word? Was it fulfilled in some past decade or era or does it still determine our future? And if it does, would it not be wise to adjust our living to it? Or indeed, could it not furnish us with a hope for the future we do not presently have in our dark circumstances?

In short, though the prophetic writings must be read within the context of their historical situations—indeed, though they cannot properly be understood apart from such specific contexts—their embedment in the actual life of Israel does not minimize their relevance for us. We are dealing with the same God, who continues to work out for human life the plan he partially revealed through his prophets. And perhaps the ways of living and trusting required of Israel in the sixth century b.c. are analogous to those ways of action and faith required of us by God in our decade. We cannot be sure until we have searched the prophetic oracles. One thing is certain: if we would be wise and live realistically in the twentieth century, then search them we must.

The Authors and Date of Trito-Isaiah

Having said all that, the clinker in the mix is our ignorance of Trito-Isaiah's situation. In fact, we do not even know for sure who wrote Isaiah 56-66. As they now stand in our Bible, those eleven chapters are part of the whole which is attributed to Isaiah of Jerusalem (1:1) and which therefore is to be dated from about 745 to 701 b.c. There is no other superscription to be found throughout the sixty-six chapters which would countermand such dating or attribution of authorship. Therefore some conservative scholars view the entire Isaiah corpus as the developing work of one prophet.

There are, however, many internal indications of the historical setting of the various parts of the Isaiah book, and since the eighteenth century, chapters 40-66 (and sometimes chapters 34-35) have been routinely separated from chapters 1-33. (Chapters 36-39 parallel 2 Kings 18:13—20:19, with some differences.) In Isaiah 1-33, Judah and Israel are still in existence as separate kingdoms, and their rulers are referred to by name (Uzziah, Ahaz, Hezekiah, Pekah). Assyria is the dominant power on the world scene. Various events of the eighth century B.C., such as the death of Uzziah, the Syro-Ephraimitic crisis, the fall of the northern kingdom, the siege of Ashdod, and the invasion of Sennacherib are clearly referred to. In Isaiah 40-66, on the other hand, Assyria has fallen, and its successor Babylon is about to fall. Cyrus the Great, king of Persia, is twice mentioned by name. The Jews are in exile in Babylonia, and Jerusalem with its temple, and Judah lie in ruins.

In addition, the forms of prophetic speech, the style of the language, and the theological outlook of chapters 40-66 (34-35) differ radically from those in chapters 1-33. All but the most ultra-conservative scholars are convinced that a second Isaiah corpus, made up of chapters 40-66 (perhaps plus 34-35) must be separated from Isaiah 1-33 and attributed to an anonymous prophet writing probably in Babylonia some years after 550 B.C.

But is there a Third Isaiah? Are 40-66 a unity, or are chapters 56-66 also to be separated from chapters 40-55? The German scholar Bernhard Duhm was the first to suggest, in 1892, that such a division was to be made. Once again on the basis of historical references, and on literary and theological grounds, Duhm maintained that chapters 56-66 were the work of a later prophet living in Jerusalem shortly before the time of Nehemiah and roughly contemporary with Malachi, that is, about 450 B.C.

Clearly, the historical situation mirrored in chapters 56-66 is different from that in chapters 40-55. The setting is Jerusalem, some of the exiles have returned from Babylonia, and the book portrays the miserable conditions, the difficulties, and the quarrels taking place in the postexilic Jerusalem community. At the same time, the cult is much more the focus of thought, an apocalyptic note has crept into the theology, the mood has shifted from the excited expectation of the exiles to that of the returnees' bitter disappointment and acrimonious disputes.

Is this development the continuation of Second Isaiah's prophecy? There is much in chapters 56-66 that sounds like his work, especially chapters 60-62. Walter Zimmerli, in his essay "Zur Sprache Tritojesajas," has shown that there are even word for word citations from Deutero-Isaiah in some passages in Trito-Isaiah, as well as new or free usages of Deutero-Isaiah's forms and themes. Consequently, many responsible scholars have maintained that chapters 56-66 are also the work of Second Isaiah, or that they contain the words of Second Isaiah, spoken after the return from exile and supplemented by the utterances of disciples. As John Bright put it, "The great prophet would surely have made the return—had he been able so much as to crawl!"[1] There are, however, other more satisfactory explanations to be given for the resemblances between Second and Third Isaiah than that of common authorship, and these can explain the differences between the two works as well. But first of all, the reader must understand the way the prophetic books came into being.

The popular stereotype of prophetic authorship pictures a lonely figure, receiving the Word of God in a vision or dream or from a voice out of heaven, writing it down, and then delivering it—thus the fundamentalist claims that the prophet has had dictated to him the inerrant Word of God.

Certainly many of the prophetic books in the Old Testament grew out of the preaching of an individual, whose words formed its core. And the revelation given to that individual came in ways which defy our understanding (cf. Amos 7:14-15; Hos. 1:2; Isa. 6:1-12; Jer. 1:4-10, 11-12, 13-14; Ezek. 1:1—3:15, etc.). We simply do not know what it means when Isaiah says, "The Lord of hosts

---

1. *The History of Israel,* 3rd ed. Philadelphia: Westminster, 1981, p. 367n63.

has revealed himself in my ears" (22:14), or when Amos says, "The Lord God showed me" (7:1, 4, 7). Ezekiel's claim that the Lord "put forth the form of a hand, and took me by a lock of my head; and the Spirit lifted me up between earth and heaven, and brought me in visions of God to Jerusalem" (8:3) is a statement totally alien to our experience. Indeed, in our society we confine persons who make such claims to mental institutions! But the prophets were not mentally unbalanced. Their words stood the test of time and revealed the course and purpose of Israel's history and were validated by their fulfillment in the life of the people of God.

Few of the prophets wrote down their own words, however, although Isaiah 40-55, with its careful literary construction, may be the exception. We know from Jeremiah's biography that he dictated his oracles to his scribe, Baruch (36:1-4, 32). But usually a prophet's words were remembered and recorded by groups of his disciples and followers (cf. Isa. 8:16). Often brief oracles were passed on orally from person to person (cf. Jer. 26:17-18), or small collections of oracles were written down and treasured by various sympathetic groups. Thus most prophetic books, including Trito-Isaiah, betray within them the presence of smaller, earlier collections (cf. Isa. 60-62; 65). These smaller collections were then gradually assembled together, sometimes on the basis of a common theme (cf. Jer. 23:9-40 on the prophets, or 21:11—22:30 on the kings), sometimes by catchwords linking together separate oracles, sometimes by similar dates of the separate oracles (e.g., Jer. 1-3 are from that prophet's early preaching).

Moreover, these disciples and followers who collected and preserved the prophets' oracles sometimes added material of their own or altered the prophetic preaching to make it relevant to a later time or different situation (cf. the addition of the oracles on Tyre, Edom, and Judah in Amos 1:3—2:16). For example, it has long been recognized that within the Book of Jeremiah there is a large block of material which frames that prophet's words in the stereotyped language and theology of the Deuteronomic movement that surfaced in the reform of King Josiah in 622 B.C. (cf. 2 Kings 22-23; 2 Chron. 34-35). We used to think that such Deuteronomic material did not reflect Jeremiah's own positions, but it is now becoming more and more evident that there was a reform group in Judah, made up of Levites, some nobles, and a group of prophets, who, under the opportunity afforded by Josiah's independence from Assyria, acted to restore the ancient Mosaic covenant faith to the southern kingdom.[2] It is also likely that Jeremiah was a member of this reform group, that the group wrote down much of his preaching, and that the Deuteronomistic portions of the Jeremiah corpus therefore preserve his authentic positions, though they frame them in stereotyped Deuteronomistic language. This group will become exceedingly important later on in our discussion of the authorship of Trito-Isaiah.

The main point to note here, however, is that each prophetic book was the product of the efforts of a small group or community which championed the prophet's cause or which shared a common theology reflected also in the prophet's preaching.[3] In the case of the Isaiah corpus of chapters 1-66, the community which formed around Isaiah of Jerusalem in the eighth century B.C. was evidently vital enough to become the beginning of an Isaianic "school" that lasted for at least two centuries, through the experience of the exile and of the return. This Isaianic school was responsible for preserving and assembling Isaiah 1-39, and then for adding first chapters 40-55, and for assembling and then adding chapters 56-66. There was a theology characteristic of the school throughout its existence, and yet the school also modified its views and emphases from time to time, as Israel's historical situation changed and as new prophetic leaders of the school came forward with a new Word from the Lord. The resemblances

---

2. See my Proclamation Commentary, *Deuteronomy, Jeremiah,* Philadelphia: Fortress, 1979.

3. In dealing with the inspiration of the Scriptures, one therefore has to relate that inspiration to the work of these small communities as well as to the work of individual prophets and writers. For a full discussion see P. J. Achtemeier, *The Inspiration of Scripture,* Philadelphia: Westminster, 1980.

between Deutero- and Trito-Isaiah are much more marked than those of First Isaiah with either of them. And yet an overriding emphasis on the sovereign rule of the Holy One of Israel binds together the thought of the three distinctive works.

Certainly First and Second Isaiah preserve the words of two individual prophets, who were active in eighth century Jerusalem and sixth century B.C. Babylonia respectively. The question is, Does Trito-Isaiah also preserve the preaching of an individual prophet, who can be so certainly dated? Many scholars have said no, characterizing the work as the compilation of oracles from various authors, dating from the eighth or sixth to the third century B.C. Other scholars who have opted for a single author of the work have been unable to agree on the date of his activity, placing him at various times in the sixth or fifth century B.C.

Much of this uncertainty has been due to the fact that we do not know a great deal about the period after the destruction of Jerusalem in 587 B.C. The only nonprophetic biblical source for the postexilic period through the fifth century B.C. is the concluding portion of the Chronicler's work found in Ezra-Nehemiah, and many details of life in Babylonia and Judah during the exile and after can only be gleaned from postexilic writings of the prophets themselves. We are therefore in the position of trying to date a prophetic work on the basis of evidence gleaned only from prophetic works. Uncertainty is bound to result.

Yet, there are ways of assessing the unity and authorship of a work, on the basis of its language, structure, and thought. I believe that Trito-Isaiah is essentially a unified product of the Isaianic school of 538-515 B.C., that there probably were individual prophets from whose preaching its words were collected, but that these prophets understood themselves as members of an elect community that had taken over the role of the Suffering Servant of Second Isaiah. Trito-Isaiah is therefore a communal expression, exhibiting the variety characteristic of any community, and yet one in its basic themes, structure, and vocabulary. This view will be supported, I believe, in the exposition of the book which follows.

The Community Behind Trito-Isaiah

Before proceeding to the exposition, it will be helpful to examine more fully this Isaianic community out of which Trito-Isaiah came. Who was this group responsible for this prophetic corpus? What were their purposes in preserving and assembling this work? What was their relation to the larger postexilic community?

Trito-Isaiah itself gives us a clear picture of the small community from which it sprang. It was an oppressed and outcast group (cf. 56:8; 57:1; 63:16), which had no power or status in the larger community (cf. 57:15; 66:2). Indeed, it was rejected by society at large because of its religious stance (66:5) and not considered to belong in the covenant community (63:16). It is possible that it included foreigners and eunuchs among its number (cf. 56:1-8), but it certainly saw itself as the real Israel (65:8-16), which was righteous (57:1), chosen (65:9, 15, 22), the true servants of Yahweh (65:8, 9, 13, 14), his holy people (63:18). It was the group that truly loved Jerusalem (66:10), that revered Yahweh's Word (66:2, 5), that took refuge in Yahweh (57:13) and that disdained the worship of all other gods. As such, it was under active attack from adversaries within the larger community (57:1; 59:15; 66:5), whom it considered to be idolatrous forsakers of Yahweh (57:3-13; 59:5-8), enemies of his (66:14), bringing his wrath upon the whole community (58:1-14; 59:1-15).

In short, the community behind Trito-Isaiah was an embattled group, and Trito-Isaiah is a polemical document, defending the cause of a righteous group and pronouncing judgment on the ways of its unrighteous adversaries. Israel is no longer one people in Trito-Isaiah, but a community split down the middle—divided between loyalty and apparent lack of loyalty to Yahweh its Lord.

There are some further clues in Trito-Isaiah to the concrete issues lying behind such schism. In 66:21, Yahweh declares that he will take some from the foreign nations for Levitical priests (not priests and Levites, as in the rsv), and in 56:1-8, foreigners and even eunuchs will be welcomed at the temple altar. Those considered righteous by Yahweh (57:1), who keep the sabbath (56:2, 4, 6; 58:13), and who practice true fasts (cf. 58:6-12) will be his priests (cf. 61:6), to whom all the wealth of the nations will flow for a sacrifice upon Yahweh's altar (60:5-7). There is frequent mention of the temple (66:6) as the place of Yahweh's sanctuary (60:13; 63:18), as his house (56:5, 7; 60:7), holy and beautiful (64:11) and glorious (60:7), as the courts of his holiness (62:9; RSV: "courts of my sanctuary") on his holy mountain (56:7; 57:13; 65:11, 25; 66:20). When the adversaries are criticized, it is often in terms of their idolatrous and pagan worship (57:3-13; 64:7; 65:11; 66:3, 17). In other words, the interest of the community responsible for Trito-Isaiah is cultic, but its outlook is broad and universal, welcoming all faithful people to the temple, which will become "a house of prayer for all peoples" (56:7). Apparently the Trito-Isaiah community was fighting some who had narrower views regarding those worthy to worship in the temple.

However, we can define the situation even more closely than that.[4] The acceptance of foreigners as Levitical priests in 66:21 forms the closing companion piece to the similar beginning announcement in 56:1-8. In short, such acceptance is stressed. But such openness with regard to the priesthood would have been anathema to some groups in postexilic Judah. In the ideal community envisioned by Ezekiel 40-48, which is an exilic addition to that prophet's oracles, only Zadokite priests could approach the altar (Ezek. 40:46). The Levites were excluded from the priestly service of the altar and were appointed only as temple servants, the reason being given that the Levites went astray and worshiped idols (Ezek. 44:13-14). Foreigners and uncircumcised were forbidden entrance to the temple area altogether (Ezek. 44:9), in

---

4. Paul Hanson, in *The Dawn of Apocalyptic,* Philadelphia: Fortress, 1975, has led the way in illumining the situation of Trito-Isaiah. My own study has confirmed his basic position, although I am in disagreement with him on many specific points.

order to keep the sacred precincts absolutely ritually pure of all secular taints.

Similarly, in the Priestly History (P) compiled in Babylonia during the exile, 587-538 B.C., the priestly service at the altar was reserved to the Zadokite priests, with the Levites "given" to them as temple servants (Num. 3:6-10; 8:19; 18:6-7). Once again there was the charge, set forth in the story of Eli, that the Levitical priests had been unfaithful and that Yahweh had to raise up for himself "a faithful priest," namely Zadok, in the time of Solomon (1 Sam. 2:27-36; 1 Kings 2:35). After the exile, in the writings of Haggai and Zechariah, 520-518 B.C., the concern is to restore the temple, effecting the program of P and Ezekiel 40-48, installing the Zadokite high priest and Davidic prince as the leaders of the community (Hag. 2:1-5; Zech. 3:1-10), and thus ensuring Yahweh's favor and dwelling in the midst of his people.

In other words, there was during the exilic and postexilic periods, a widespread cultic tradition, which reserved the priesthood to Zadokite priests, which excluded all foreign elements from Yahweh's temple, and which thereby believed to make the community a fit dwelling place for the holy Yahweh (cf. Zech. 2:10-12).

This was not a matter of esoteric ritualism and exclusivistic pride for those who held such views. Rather it was a matter of life and death. Israel had been rejected by her God and sent into Babylonian exile for her sins against him. The question, therefore, among the exiles was how to regain Yahweh's favor, how to insure that he would never again bring his judgments upon his people. The answer of the priestly leaders of the exilic community in Babylonia was that Israel had to be cleansed of all idolatrous worship, all contact with foreign ways and influences which had led her to become like any other nation and to forfeit her life as the holy people of God (cf. Ezek. 20:32). Israel worshiped a holy God; she herself had therefore to be holy, i.e., "set apart" (Lev. 19:2). Priestly parties set out in the exilic and postexilic periods to insure such holiness through an exclusivistic and purified cult.

Trito-Isaiah comes therefore from a group which did not share such exclusivistic views, and like Deuteronomy and later portions in the Chronicler's History, it probably is the work of Levitical priests, and additionally of prophets, this time resident in Jerusalem and the small surrounding territory left to Judah after 587 B.C. If we review the history of the Levitical priesthood, such a conclusion seems all the more certain.

Up until the time of Saul, Israel's tribes were held together as a loose federation by their common loyalty to Yahweh, whose presence with them was symbolized by the ark of the covenant, kept at a central shrine. The tribes were bound to Yahweh by a covenant, and periodically they journeyed to the central shrine—at first in Shechem, later at Shiloh—to renew their covenant vows to have no other gods beside Yahweh. But Israel also worshiped Yahweh at sanctuaries throughout the land of Palestine, and apparently from the very earliest times, there were two rival priestly groups in Israel: the Aaronid priesthood, descended from Aaron (the later Zadokites) and the Mushite priesthood, descended from Moses (the later Levites).[5] It was the Mushites who served as priests at the central shrine, and who had the closest connection with Mosaic covenant theology, with the tribal federation, and with the prophetic movement which championed covenant loyalty to Yahweh. Eli at Shiloh was a Mosaic or Mushite priest.

When David moved the ark to Jerusalem, he cleverly kept intact the structure of the tribal federation, with its covenant theology, and he appointed Abiathar of the Mushite line as high priest. But with an eye to politics and the unity of his kingdom, he also appointed as co-high priest, Zadok of the Aaronid line, which had had its center in Jerusalem and Hebron. Thereby rival interests were balanced against each other. However, in the power struggle for the throne which followed David's death, the

---

5. See F. M. Cross, "The Priestly Houses of Early Israel," *Canaanite Myth and Hebrew Epic*. Cambridge: Harvard University Press, 1973, pp. 195ff. for a full discussion.

Mushite or Levitical priest, Abiathar, made the mistake of siding with Solomon's elder brother Adonijah (1 Kings 2). Solomon banished Abiathar to the Levitical city of Anathoth (the later home of the prophet Jeremiah), and made Zadok his priest (1 Kings 2:35). From that time on, Zadokite priests were closely connected with the monarchy, although Levitical priests continued to officiate at shrines throughout the country. But because the Zadokite priesthood often tended to support royalist claims to absolute power on the basis of the promise to David and in contradiction to the Mosaic covenant with Yahweh, the prophetic movement found itself increasingly set over against the Zadokites, the kings whom they served, and the cultic life of Jerusalem (cf. Amos 7:10-17; Hos. 4:4-10; Isa. 1:10-17; Jer. 26).

In 622/621 B.C., during a time of relative freedom from Assyrian power and of expanding nationalist feeling, King Josiah of Judah set about to rid his nation of all foreign influence. While some repairs were being made on the temple, a copy of the Book of Deuteronomy (including at least chapters 5-26 and 28) was found, undoubtedly having been placed there by the reform party of Levites, nobles, and prophets of which we spoke earlier. Deuteronomy stipulated that all worship was to be centralized in Jerusalem, that all local cult sites which had become so corrupted by Canaanite baalistic practices were to be done away, and that the power of the throne was to be subordinated to the Mosaic covenant law. In short, Deuteronomy was an attempt to return Judah to the ancient covenant faith championed by the prophets and especially by the prophet Jeremiah at the time. Josiah took the Levitical preaching of Deuteronomy to heart, removed all pagan influences and priests, bound the nation to Deuteronomy's laws with a covenant ceremony, and sealed the whole with a celebration of the Passover (2 Kings 22-23; 2 Chron. 34-35). It was a throughgoing attempt to make Judah, so corrupted by heathen influences, once again faithful to God.

Deuteronomy's centralization of worship in Jerusalem meant, however, that the Levitical priests, who had served at shrines throughout the countryside, were without jobs. But Levites are given a prominent place in Deuteronomy, being regarded as true priests (18:1-8 et passim) and as the custodians of the Torah (17:18; 31:9, 24ff.). Those who lived outside of Jerusalem were to be allowed to come to Jerusalem and to minister at the altar in the temple. In short, Deuteronomy placed Levites and Zadokite priests on the same level, while at the same time devaluing the absolutist claims of the throne and making the Davidic king also subject to the Deuteronomic covenant law (Deut. 17:14-20).

A brief notice in 2 Kings 23:9 reflects the fact that the Zadokite Jerusalem priesthood resisted the Deuteronomic effort to install Levites as priests in the temple. The result was that many Levites continued to live in the countryside, and Deuteronomy had to direct that charity be given to them along with the widows and orphans (Deut. 12:19; 14:27-29; 16:11, 14; 26:12-13). The Levites at the end of the seventh century B.C. continued as lower-class clergy.

When Jerusalem fell to the Babylonians in July 587 B.C., the tables were turned. The city with its temple and palace was plundered and put to the torch, its walls were broken down, and the leading ecclesiastical, military, and civil officials were hauled before Nebuchadnezzar at Riblah and executed (2 Kings 25:8-21; Jer. 52). In addition, some 832 leading men and their families, according to Jer. 52:29, were exiled to Babylonia. Jer. 52:30 reports that the total number exiled in the deportations of 597, 587, and 582 B.C. was 4600 adult males, plus their families, which means that Jerusalem and Judah were by no means denuded of population. But certainly thousands had died in battle or of starvation and disease (cf. Lam. 2:11-12, 19-21; 4:9-10), and many others had fled for their lives and become refugees (cf. Jer. 42-43). From a population of some 250,000 in the eighth century, it is estimated that Judah was reduced to less than 20,000 residents.[6] Certainly most of the Zadokite priesthood was exiled. Those remaining in

---

6. Bright, pp. 365f.

the land were the poor, some prophets, including the prophet Jeremiah (Jer. 39:11-14; 40:1-6), some leaders of the Deuteronomic reform movement, including Gedaliah who was appointed governor of the province (Jer. 40:5), and—the Levitical priests! Judging by the lists of those who returned from exile, few Levites were carried into Babylonia, because they had had little power in the Judean community (cf. Ezra 2:36-42; Neh. 7:39-45). Instead, the Levites remained in the ruined land.

The Levitical priests apparently carried on their sacred duties, despite the desolation of Jerusalem and its surroundings. We know from Jer. 41:5-6 that sacrifices continued to be offered at the site of the ruined temple altar. In addition, there were undoubtedly public ceremonies of repentance and fasting conducted on the temple grounds (Zech. 7:1-5; 8:18-19; the book of Lamentations may have been used in these ceremonies). And it could only have been Levitical priests who officiated at these cultic occasions. The exile of the Zadokite priesthood restored the rights of the Levites!

In Babylonian exile, however, the Zadokite priesthood was busy formulating the history and laws that were to serve as patterns for the ideal community upon the return from exile. The Priestly History and Ezekiel were put in their final forms, both of them containing scathing denunciations of the Levitical priests (cf. Num. 16:8-11) and especially of those Levites remaining in Jerusalem and Judah (cf. Ezek. 33:23-29; 44). At the same time, the Deuteronomic History (Deut.-2 Kings), which incorporated the Book of Deuteronomy and which had originally ended with the account of the reign of Josiah, was expanded to include the account of the exile and a final notice of the freeing of the Davidic heir in Babylon (2 Kings 25:27-30), thus joining the hope for the future to the promise to David.

After the fall of Babylonia to Cyrus of Persia in 539 B.C., the priestly leaders of the exiled Jews gained the permission of Cyrus to return to Palestine and to reinstitute the cultic life of the nation (Ezra 1:2-4; 6:3-5). Cyrus was one of the most enlightened rulers of ancient times, allowing subject people as far as possible to enjoy cultural autonomy and to pursue their own religious interests under the guidance of native princes. However, Cyrus also undoubtedly wanted his Palestinian flank secure against Egyptian expansionism, and he agreed to the return and rebuilding of the Jewish temple by the priestly party in exchange for Jewish loyalty to him.

The initial return under Sheshbazzar accomplished little (Ezra 1:5-11). It may be that it was he and not the later Zerubbabel who restored the altar (Ezra 3:3). Apparently he and his group laid the foundations of the temple (Ezra 5:16); but the accounts are now confused with those of the work of Zerubbabel, and it is very difficult to know what actually took place. Certainly there was opposition to the work (Ezra 3:3; 4:4), not only from the Samaritans to the north, from whose territory the province of Judah was removed, but probably also from the Levitical and reform elements left in Judah.

Judah's cult was not restored until a larger group of exiles, led by the davidide Zerubbabel, returned to Palestine, probably about 530 B.C., and were finally inspired by the prophets Haggai and Zechariah, against all opposition, to renew the work on the temple in 520 B.C., completing the project in the spring of 515 B.C. With the dedication of the temple, the installation of Zerubbabel as governor and of Joshua the Zadokite as the high priest, the priestly Zadokite party once again asserted its supremacy over the life of Judah, and the Levites had to be content to serve as lesser clergy in the restored cult.

The dissatisfaction of the Levitical priests with such an arrangement is mirrored even much later in the Chronicler's History of about 400 B.C., a document whose additions are at pains to glorify the role of the Levites, attributing their equal status in the cult to the organization of the temple worship by the great King David himself (1 Chron. 24). In actuality, the Zadokites remained the dominant group and controlled the high priesthood until the second century B.C.

It is in the midst of this long struggle between the Levitical-reform-Deuteronomic-prophetic group and the priestly-exclusivistic-Zadokite party that Trito-Isaiah belongs, specifically in the period between 538 and 515 B.C.

Trito-Isaiah therefore has a twofold background of tradition: that of the Isaianic school reaching back to the eighth century B.C., and that of the Deuteronomic reform school which is so evident at the end of the seventh century B.C. in the preaching of the prophet Jeremiah. Just how and at what point these two prophetic traditions joined forces cannot now be fully traced. Certainly both Isaiah of Jerusalem and Jeremiah attacked the Zadokite temple cult and absolutized monarchy on the basis of the ancient covenant traditions of the central sanctuary at Shiloh (cf. Isa. 8:5-8; Jer. 7:1-15), and it may have been that the school of Isaiah and the members of the Deuteronomic reform movement found themselves natural allies in the turbulent last years of Judah's history. Certainly later tradition confused the two groups: 2 Chron. 36:22-23 alludes to Second Isaiah's predictions about Cyrus and attributes them to Jeremiah. Jer. 33:14-26 reiterates the Isaianic promise of a righteous Branch from David (cf. Isa. 11:1; Jer. 23:5-6), but then joins it with the promise of an eternal Levitical priesthood. Somewhere along the line, the Isaiah school and the Levitical-Deuteronomic reformers joined forces, and this took place before the time of Trito-Isaiah, because that book reflects both lines of tradition, as we shall see in the exposition.

One word needs to be added regarding a new approach to the interpretation of the Isaiah books that has been set forth by Brevard Childs in his *Introduction to the Old Testament as Scripture* (Philadelphia: Fortress, 1979). Childs maintains that because Second and Third Isaiah lack all historical superscriptions and have been joined to First Isaiah, they have been removed from their historical contexts in the final shape of the canon and are to be interpreted as a spiritualized and eternal Word of Isaiah's God. In short, for Childs, all of this preceding discussion of the historical context of Trito-Isaiah makes no difference. But as was stated at the beginning of this introduction, the Word of God is spoken to very specific situations in Israel's life, and we really do not understand that Word unless we know the situation to which it is speaking. Time and again, as we shall see in the exposition, the words of Trito-Isaiah can be understood properly only against their historical background. It is the Word in the context of that specific background, then, which the expositor must relate to our life. To be sure, it would be easier to spiritualize the words of the Bible and to apply them directly to ourselves, but it would not be wiser, because the Word of God really has been spoken into history and not into some eternal realm. God really has broken in to time and space, to bring us his salvation. It is that fact that makes the biblical message good news.

Some Thoughts on Studying Trito-Isaiah

Most ministers and lay people in the church are used to dipping into the Bible only at isolated points, in order to prepare a sermon, to plan a Sunday school lesson, to present a devotional, to gain spiritual guidance in some particular moment. But by approaching the Bible in such a piecemeal fashion, we never really hear what it says. Trito-Isaiah is now presented to us in our Bibles as an integral whole, carefully planned and shaped by the sixth century B.C. community which assembled it. Its thought unfolds in an ordered structure and, I believe, in a chronological sequence that gradually reveals its message. Only by working our way through that structure and sequence, from beginning to end, can we really grasp what Third Isaiah is all about.

It should also be noted that when we approach the Bible in a piecemeal fashion, we miss all the fun. There is something exciting about the work of biblical scholarship—about starting out with a blank piece of paper and gradually, step by step, translating and plumbing and explaining the meaning of an ancient text. It is like watching a terribly important ancient scroll, sealed for centuries, being unrolled inch by inch. A picture of actual life before God begins to emerge into clarity.

People would therefore be better off if they could dispense with commentaries and Bible "helps" and unroll each biblical scroll for themselves, duplicating in their own individual or group study the process that every biblical scholar goes through. Then they themselves would be wrestling with the text and experiencing its emergence into meaning. However, most persons are not trained for such a task and need the information and guidance which biblical scholarship affords. And that, of course, is the principal purpose of scholarly study of the Bible: it helps the church confront the actual meaning of the biblical text.

There is no reason, however, why the persons who use this volume to aid them in their study of Third Isaiah cannot experience something of the excitement that I have known in the writing of this book. They can recapture that excitement if they too work their way, step by step, through the message of Trito-Isaiah. To be sure, that involves detailed and careful study, but there is no other way fully to hear God's Word spoken through Third Isaiah. It cannot be grasped in general, but only by painstaking examination of all of its nuances and particularities. Then it speaks forth, fully and clearly, and its meaning is rich indeed.

To aid the reader in this process, the Hebrew text of each passage will be translated. Words not found in the Hebrew text will be enclosed in brackets: [ ]. Alternate and literal meanings of the text will be put in parentheses: ( ). Additions to the text which should be omitted will be enclosed in double parentheses: (( )).

The reader should carefully go through and study the translation of each passage before going on to the comment on it, making a thorough effort to discern the passage's meaning and audience. This then should be checked against the discussion given of the passage.

In connection with each prophetic passage or oracle, we will look at the form of the text, at its context, its internal structure, its emphases and audience, in the attempt to discern the text's meaning in Israel and what it says about the living God. Often we will refer to similar passages in other biblical books, or we will indicate, by biblical references, where the prophet earlier said much the same thing. These biblical references should be looked up and read as the reader proceeds, because they will show the unity of Trito-Isaiah and the way its message gradually unfolds. In addition, the biblical references will reveal the relation of Trito-Isaiah's message to the Isaianic-Levitical-Deuteronomic schools, as well as to the message of other biblical witnesses. Similarly, references to books later than Trito-Isaiah and to the New Testament will help the reader understand how the message of Third Isaiah was used in later Israel, in the accounts of Jesus' activity, and in the New Testament church. Trito-Isaiah is but part of an ongoing biblical revelation, begun long before the sixth century B.C. and continued well after it. Only by reading Trito-Isaiah's message in the total canonical context, can we fully understand its meaning and its importance in God's two thousand year-long revelation of himself to his covenant people. And only by understanding the words of this book can its message, preached so long ago, become the present Word of God for us today.

Unfolding the Message

PART I Isaiah 56-59

Isaiah 56:1-8

1 Thus says Yahweh:
        Be stewards of (guard/keep)
    justice and do faithfulness (lit: righteousness),
    for near is my salvation to come,
        and my deliverance (lit: righteousness) to be revealed.
2 Happy (blessed) is the person who does this
        and the one who holds it fast,
    who keeps the sabbath from profanation,
        and who guards his hand from doing any evil.

———

3 Let not the foreigner—
        the one who joins himself to Yahweh—say,
    "Yahweh will surely separate me
        from his people."
    And let not the eunuch say,
        "Behold! I am a tree that has dried up!"
4   For thus says Yahweh:
    "To the eunuchs who keep my sabbaths,
    who choose those things I desire,
        and who are holding fast my covenant,

5   I will give in my house
        and within my walls a place (monument) and a name
    that are better than sons and daughters.
        An everlasting name I will give to them
        that shall not be cut off."

        ———————

6   To the foreigners who join themselves
        to Yahweh to minister to him
        and to love the name of Yahweh,
    to be servants to him—
        all those who keep the sabbath from profanation
        and who are holding fast my covenant:
7   "I will bring them to my holy mountain,
        and I will make them glad in my house of prayer.
    Their burnt offerings and their sacrifices
        will be a delight to me upon my altar,
    for my house shall be called
        a house of prayer for all peoples,"
8   is the oracle of the Lord Yahweh,
        who is gathering the outcasts of Israel.
    "I will gather still others to those already gathered."

< *1* > The passage picks up the announcement of Second
Isaiah before it, and renews the promise: Yahweh's salvation of
his people is near (cf. 46:13; 51:5)! To those who have returned
to a ruined Jerusalem after 538 B.C. and to those who shortly will
return, to those who see nothing but devastation all around them,
to those who are struggling to make ends meet and to find some
reason for living, even under the hand of the Persian conqueror,
Third Isaiah sets v 1 like a banner over its whole pronouncement:
the Word of God still stands; deliverance is very near (cf. 40:8;
55:10-11). The word for deliverance is literally "righteousness,"
but "deliverance" is the meaning of that term here. "Righteousness" is, in the Bible, always the fulfillment of the demands of a
relationship, and in his deliverance of his chosen people, Yahweh
fulfills his covenant with them. Similarly, in v 1c, persons are

righteous before God when they are faithful to him, because it is such faithfulness that Yahweh asks of them in his relationship with them.

We have here a form of a prophetic oracle known as a salvation oracle. Its main thrust throughout is the announcement of good news, and it reiterates one of the two great motifs of salvation promised by Second Isaiah. That prophet had proclaimed that the exiles would return to Palestine, experiencing a new exodus-redemption and guidance through the wilderness more glorious than those that Israel had known when Yahweh first redeemed her out of Egypt (cf. 43:14-21; 51:9-11; 52:3-12; 41:17-20). But that was not the most important part of Second Isaiah's announcement. His most important good news was that Yahweh would return to his people. For a brief moment forsaken by God for her sin (54:4-8), Judah would nevertheless be able to lift up her eyes and to peer out over the desert and see Yahweh, the Holy One of Israel, coming once again to dwell in her midst, bringing her exiled children with him as he came (40:9-11; 52:8). That was finally the meaning of "salvation" for Israel—the return of Yahweh to be with her (cf. 41:10, 13-14; 43:5; 51:12-16; 52:6)—because when Yahweh is present, there is nothing to be afraid of. With Yahweh are all power, all goodness, all fullness of life. Yahweh's presence with his people makes the difference between life or death (cf. 45:7). Everything hangs on whether or not he says to Israel, "My people" (cf. 40:1).

This is the salvation that commands the attention of Third Isaiah—the presence of Yahweh with his people. Obviously some of the exiles have already returned to Judah, but that does not mean that Second Isaiah's message has been fulfilled. None of the prophets, nor the New Testament, considers the return from exile to be synonymous with salvation. Salvation can be had only in the company of God, who is the Creator and Author of all life and good. Unless he reestablishes the covenant bond, life on earth remains a living death, no matter what its circumstances. The rebuilding of the ruined temple and city and land are not the most important for Trito-Isaiah, but rather God's rebuilding of Israel's broken relationship with him.

In this first poem of the prophetic corpus, therefore, the prophetic community combines its salvation oracle with a prophetic torah or teaching, in order to instruct the people about salvation. Yahweh is coming. The question therefore is, "To whom will he come?" And the answer is twofold in v 1. First, Yahweh will come to those who are stewards of justice, which means those who establish Yahweh's order in the community's life, according to his revealed commandments. Second, Yahweh will come to those who are righteous, that is, faithful to their relationship with God in all their dealings.

< 2 > Special emphasis is here put upon Sabbath observance because such observance had become, along with circumcision, a mark of the faithful Jew living among the heathen after the fall of Judah (cf. Exod. 31:12-17P; Jer. 17:19-27; Ezek. 20:12, 20). But to "be stewards of justice and do faithfulness" in v 1 also certainly included obedience to the law of Deuteronomy, to whose commands Trito-Isaiah envisions Judah to be responsible. That means much more than legalistic obedience to the law however. Throughout this poem, the persons to be saved are those who "hold fast" faithfulness to Yahweh (vv 2, 4, 6), who "join" themselves to the Lord (vv 3, 6), who "choose" those things that Yahweh desires (v 4), who "love" his name (v 6). Trito-Isaiah reflects here the inward nature of covenant faithfulness, so important also in Deuteronomy. Such faithfulness is a matter of the heart and will; of conscious, ethical, daily wrestling to follow God's ways; of total and willing love for the God who has first loved Israel; of cleaving to God, holding him fast, in a fellowship unbroken by any circumstances (cf. Deut. 6:4-9; 10:12-21, et passim). Any person who so loves God and is faithful to him, says Third Isaiah in the wisdom formula of v 2, is the person who will have life in its fullness, i.e., who will be "blessed," because God will be present with him.

< 3-7 > Trito-Isaiah knows of the plans being formulated among
the priestly groups in exile—plans to reconstitute the new postexilic Israel on the basis of exclusive cultic purity, under the stipulations of the Priestly Code.[1] Under the P Code, the service at the
altar would be limited to an elite Zadokite priestly hierarchy (cf.
Num. 18:6-7; 3:5-10; 8:19; Ezek. 40:45-46), while sections of
Ezekiel 40-48 would exclude foreigners from even worshiping in
the temple (Ezek. 44:6-9) (see the Introduction). Indeed, in contradiction to the words of Jeremiah (ch. 29), those in exile were
claiming that they alone remained faithful to God, while those
in the land were idolatrous and had been rejected by the Lord
(cf. Ezek. 11:14-23; Ezra 6:21). In a daring reformulation of the
teaching of Deut. 23:1-8, Trito-Isaiah therefore proclaims that *all*
faithful people who love Yahweh and cling to him will be welcomed in the rebuilt temple, and may themselves, in a priesthood
of all believers (cf. Exod. 19:6), offer their sacrifices upon Yahweh's altar. Holiness before the Lord is not a matter of exclusivistic and ritualistic purity, as the Zadokite hierarchy would main-
tain, but a matter of holding fast to the covenant God. And it
is not the priests alone who are holy, but all of Yahweh's covenant
people, in accordance with the teachings of Deuteronomy (cf.
Deut. 7:6; 26:19; 28:8; Jer. 2:3). By including even eunuchs
among those to be welcomed into Yahweh's house (cf. Acts 8:27-
38), Trito-Isaiah reinterprets Deut. 23:1 to apply to his new
situation.[2]

It was not unusual for a prophet to reinterpret the law, despite
the stipulations of Deut. 4:2 and 12:32. On the basis of a new
Word from God, Isaiah of Jerusalem had earlier reinterpreted
cultic law (1:10-17), and he had extended the first commandment
to apply to foreign alliances and military weapons (31:1), just as
later, Jesus of Nazareth radically reinterpreted many legal pre-
scriptions (cf. Matt. 5:17-48).

1. Jer. 29 shows quite clearly that communications were readily maintained between Babylonia and Jerusalem.
2. Some captives of war who were servants of Babylonian masters during the exile,
were castrated to prevent their exercise of sexual prowess.

In its reinterpretation of the law, Trito-Isaiah was not, however, introducing totally new thoughts. It spoke out of the universalism of Deutero-Isaiah (cf. 42:1-4; 44:5; 49:6; 45:22-23) and of the Isaianic school (cf. 2:2-4; 14:1; 19:19-25). And indeed, preexilic Israel had never excluded the worshiping foreigner from the temple—i.e., one who was not a resident alien but a stranger in the land (cf. Exod. 12:48-49; Num. 15:14-16). From the beginning, Israel's faith looked toward the blessing of all the families of the earth (Gen. 12:3), and the Suffering Servant of Second Isaiah, i.e., Israel itself, was called to give its life for the sake of the foreign nations (52:13—53:12). Yahweh wished to restore all peoples to the good life that he had intended for them in the creation of the earth; such had always been Israel's understanding of the plan of God. The question in Trito-Isaiah's time, however, was how to accomplish that plan. The Zadokite priestly hierarchy maintained that the way to its realization lay through Israel's exclusivity. Thus, in the fifth century B.C., after the time of Trito-Isaiah, the priestly law was put into effect, all marriages with foreigners were forbidden, and Israel withdrew into itself as an exclusive and legalistic community (cf. Neh. 10:28-31; ch. 13; Ezra 9-10; 2 Chron. 13:10-12). But in the time between 538 and 515 B.C., Trito-Isaiah announced a wideness of the mercy of God which would welcome all outcasts < 8 > all foreigners, all rejected peoples to his house, the temple, which was to be called a house of prayer for all peoples (cf. Mark 11:17 and pars.).

One response was asked: that Yahweh be loved as he had loved them, in faithfulness and ethical obedience. Then the eunuch who could have no children to perpetuate his name—the only form of immortality known in Israel—would be given a place in Yahweh's temple when it was rebuilt; and his name would be remembered there forever among the ranks of the faithful (cf. Gen. 12:2 on "name"). Then the foreigner without a home would find himself no longer a stranger, but a member of a holy community rejoicing "before the Lord" on Zion's holy hill. Yahweh was gradually gathering the "outcasts," his chosen people to him (cf. Isa. 11:12). He would gather many more who heretofore had never dreamed they could be included, but who would nevertheless become his, because they loved him and held fast to his covenant will for their lives (cf. John 10:16).

Yahweh was coming to be with his own—that promise still held good: therefore keep his commandments and cling faithfully to him. In other words, the faithful were to be obedient not in order that Yahweh might come, but because he was in fact coming. The initiative was with Yahweh. Obedient faith was to be the response to his act, and it was a response possible to all peoples, of whatever circumstance. Such was the broad mercy and undimmed hope Trito-Isaiah announced to those living in the midst of Judah's ruins, and to those of mixed background who were straggling toward Palestine, not sure of what awaited them.

Isaiah 56:9-12

9 "All you beasts of the field,
      come to devour!
      All you beasts in the forest!"
10 His watchmen are blind.
      All of them do not know.
    All of them are dumb dogs;
      they are not able to bark—
    dreaming, lying down,
      loving to slumber.
11 And the dogs have strong appetites;
      they are never satiated (lit: they do not know fullness).
    The shepherds also
      do not know understanding.
    All of them to their own paths have turned,
      each to his own unjust gain, one and all.
12 "Come!" [they say], "let us buy wine,
      and let us get drunk on strong drink;
    and tomorrow will be like this.
      [No, it will be] even better!"

This prophetic oracle of judgment has so many similarities to invectives found in First Isaiah (5:11-12, 20-23; 28:7-10; 29:9-12), Micah (3:5-8, 9-12), Jeremiah (6:13-15; 12:7-13), and Ezekiel (34:1-10), as well as to conditions pictured in the time of Nehemiah (5:1-13, 15; 13:4-9), that it and its companion piece in 57:1-13 have been dated as belonging "certainly" (Westermann) in preexilic times or equally as certainly, late in postexilic times. But the situation reflected here is probably that found in Judah shortly after the return of the first exiles under the leadership of Sheshbazzar, who came with the blessing of the Persian government and of the exilic Zadokite hierarchy to begin the restoration of the temple (Ezra 1:2-11; 6:3-5). The "watchmen" in the poem are prophets who accompanied the returnees (cf. Jer. 6:17; Ezek. 3:17; 33:1-9; Jer. 29:1, 15, 20-23), the "shepherds" are Sheshbazzar and his officials (cf. Jer. 10:21; 23:1; Nah. 3:18; Ezek. 34:1-10), including some priests (cf. Ezra 1:5).

< 9 > The oracle has often been extended to 57:2 or to 57:13, but we have an opportunity here to see how the internal structure of a Hebrew poem reveals its limits. It is framed by the imperative "come," in vv 9 and 12. Yahweh speaks in v 9; the leaders of the community speak in v 12, and the contrast between Yahweh's speech and that of the leaders yields the main motif of the poem, namely, the difference between Yahweh's ways and those of the returnees.

< 10-11 > Three times it is emphasized of the leaders that "they do not know" (vv 10b, 11b, 11d). The indictment against them (vv 10-11) reaches its climax in v 11e: "all of them to their own paths have turned." This turning is then further defined in terms of selfish gain (11f), with the indictment made inclusive by the constant emphasis on "all" (10b, 10c, 11e) and the final "one and all" (11f). In short, Trito-Isaiah is here stating a variation on Isa. 55:8-9: "My thoughts are not your thoughts, neither are your ways my ways, says the Lord. For as the heavens are higher than

the earth, so are my ways higher than your ways and my thoughts than your thoughts." And the prophet emphasizes this disparity between the leaders' thoughts and Yahweh's by contrasting their sayings; even while Yahweh calls for the beasts to devour the unguarded flock, the leaders call for strong drink, imagining that they are now in control of Judah and that things can only get better.

< 12 > Similarly, there is a reflection of Isa. 55:1 in the call for wine, v 12. Through the preaching of Second Isaiah, Yahweh offered the good life without money and without price. These faithless prophets and priests and civic leaders spend their money for an illusion. Their wine leads to drunkenness, Yahweh's to abundant living. Their efforts at restoration will come to naught, Yahweh's to salvation. It will do no good to rebuild the temple if Yahweh will not return to it. Without his presence, the people still will be prey to the forces of evil.

It is this of which the faithless "watchmen" have failed to warn the inhabitants of Judah, and the comparison of them to watch dogs, which lie around sleeping instead of barking, is a figure of the deepest scorn (cf. 1 Sam. 17:43; 24:14; 2 King 8:13). Dogs were never household pets in ancient Israel, but half-wild scavengers (cf. Exod. 22:31; 1 Kings 21:19, 23-24; Ps. 22:16; 68:23; Jer. 15:3; Matt. 7:6; Mark 7:28 and pars.; Luke 16:21). These prophetic "dogs" are simply telling the people what they want to hear, in order to line their own pockets with payment for their oracles (cf. Jer. 6:13-14; 23:16-17), just as the "shepherds" are not looking out for the people's interests, but are instead enjoying themselves in revelry (cf. Amos 4:1; Isa. 5:11-12; 28:1, 7-8; Mic. 2:11), singing drinking songs (such is v 12; cf. 22:13; 1 Cor. 15:32), and imagining that they have Israel's future under control. He who really controls Israel's future, however, is he who can control even the beasts, here a figure not for the foreign nations (cf. Isa. 46:11), but for scavengers eating the dead (cf. Jer. 12:9; 19:7; Ezek. 34:5; 39:17-20)—a horrible figure, perhaps used to

shock the people out of their complacency. The relationship to
Yahweh is, for Trito-Isaiah, a matter of life and death.

Isaiah 57:1-13

1   The righteous man perishes
       and there is no one
       who takes (lit: puts) it to heart.
    Men of covenant faithfulness are taken away,
       and there is no understanding [of what is happening].
    Because of evil the righteous man dies (lit: is taken away)!
2   He enters in to peace.
    Those rest in their graves (lit: upon their beds)
       who walk in [Yahweh's] straight paths (lit: straight
          before him).

       _____

3   But as for you, draw near here,
       you sons of a sorceress,
    offspring of the adulterer and the whore!
4   Against whom are you jeering?
    Against whom are you sneering
       and sticking out your tongue?
    Are you not yourselves children of rebellion,
       offspring of falsehood,
5   who are comforted [by harlotry] with the gods
       under every green tree,
    who slaughter children in the valleys,
       under clefts of the cliffs?
6   Among the smooth [stone idols] of the valley will be your
          portion;
       they, they will be your lot (destiny).
    even to them you pour out a drink-offering, you bring a
          cereal offering.
    Should I comfort [you] because of these?

       _____

7   Upon a mountain high and lofty
       you have placed your bed.

Even there you go up to offer sacrifice.
8   Upon (lit: behind) the door and the doorpost
     you have put your memorial (remembrance),
   but you have departed from me and my healing remedy.
     You have opened wide your bed,
   and you have made a bargain for yourself with them.
     You have loved their bed,
     a place you selected.
9   You journeyed to the king with oil,
     and you multiplied your perfumes.
   You sent your messengers to a distant place,
     and you bowed down (lit: lowered yourself) to Sheol.
10 With the length of your journey you were weary,
     [but] you did not say, "There is no hope."
   Your hand was strengthened;
     therefore you did not weaken.
11 But whom did you fear, and [of whom] were you afraid
     when you were false
   and did not remember me?
     You did not put [me] upon your heart.

Am I not holding my peace for a long time,
     even though you do not fear me?
12 I will [now] make known your [so-called] righteousness
     and your doings,
13 and they will not help you. When you cry out, let your
     cohorts (lit: company) deliver you!
   A wind will carry all of them away;
     a breath will blow (lit: take) them away.
   But the one who trusts (takes refuge) in me shall inherit
     the land.
   He shall possess my holy mountain.

This oracle of judgment has caused enormous difficulties for commentators, because it is so similar to condemnations of idolatry found in the writings of the preexilic prophets. It could easily belong to Hosea or Jeremiah, and the sins it details are those repeatedly condemned in the seventh century B.C. Deuteronomy. If the oracle belongs in the time of Trito-Isaiah, one wonders who is being attacked in it. Have all of these idolatrous practices continued in ruined Judah? Who, then, is the king referred to in v 9, to whom envoys are sent? Who are the "cohorts" in v 13? And who is attacking the "righteous," in vv 1 and 2?

Westermann divides the whole into three separate oracles (vv 1-2; 3-6; 7-13) and terms them, with no doubt, a preexilic collection. But the whole is held together by repeated key words and phrases ("put to heart," vv 1, 11; "bed," vv 2, 7, 8d, 8f; "to comfort," vv 5, 6), as well as by similar motifs ("remembrance," "remember," vv 8, 11; "portion," "lot," "to inherit," "to possess," vv 6, 13). In order to understand the structure and unity of Hebrew poetry, one should always look for such repetitions—part of the scholarly discipline known as rhetorical analysis.

The oracle has been joined to 56:9-12, because of the theme of "no understanding" in both 56:11 and 57:1 (cf. 42:25; 47:11). But in v 8, this poem also picks up the motif of "love" for God or the gods, reflecting 56:6, as well as the "place" of 56:5. Verse 12 ironically contrasts "righteousness" with that called for in 56:1. And both 56:7 and 57:13 are concerned with Yahweh's "holy mountain." This oracle belongs firmly among the oracles of Trito-Isaiah.

The situation in which the oracle was delivered also can be made clear. The first exiles returned under Sheshbassar and work was begun on the temple in accordance with the program of the Zadokite priestly hierarchy. Many of those who had remained in Judah during the years of the Babylonian exile sided with this program, and it is to them that this oracle is addressed. The oracle further reveals that apparently before the first return, they sent envoys with gifts to the Persian king, and Third Isaiah borrows the figure of Isa. 28:14-22 of a bargain with Sheol to characterize this trip. The envoys urged that their cultic life be restored, and they thus joined cause with the Zadokite party in exile, the "cohorts" of v 13a, i.e., their "hand was strengthened," v 10c. As a

result, and with the blessing of the Persian government, the
returning Zadokite party, along with their sympathizers in Judah,
began the restoration work. But this meant that the Levitical-
Deuteronomic party was shoved out of its place of leadership in
the ruined land, apparently sometimes violently (vv 1-2), certainly
acrimoniously (v 4). The Levitical-prophetic party became an
object of scorn and of attack, was divested of all leadership, and
was promised no place in the temple service before the altar. The
power struggle was begun anew, and the Levitical-prophetic party
was the loser.

< 1-2 > For Trito-Isaiah, this situation is one of greatest irony,
for in its view, those faithful to the covenant are the Levitical-
prophetic party members who are being rejected (v 1). It is they
who have cherished Yahweh and his commandments in their
hearts (cf. v 11), cleaving to him with that love called for in the
Deuteronomic law, while those in Judah who have sympathized
with the Zadokite cause have continued in that syncretistic worship and idolatry for which Judah was sent into exile in the first
place (cf. Jer. 44).

Paul Hanson (p. 198) has taken this oracle as a judgment on
the Zadokite hierarchy itself, and since it is inconceivable that the
returning Zadokites would engage in such flagrant violations of
the law, he interprets this oracle as an exaggerated polemic, which
is not to be taken literally. Indeed, he interprets v 7 as a reference
to the Zadokite worship in the temple on Zion, dating the oracle
after 515 B.C. (pp. 99-100).

It is not the Zadokites themselves who are condemned in this
oracle, however, but their Judean sympathizers, who have, in fact,
continued in their idolatrous ways in the land of Judah throughout the period of exile. And it is this group of Judean idolators
who now scorn and attack the Levitical-prophetic party, jeering
at them (v 4) and even bringing sentences of death upon them
(vv 1-2; for the figure of v 2, cf. Job 3:13).

< *3-4* > In reply to these attacks, the prophetic voice summons the scorners to a court trial, v 3a (cf. Isa. 41:1; 45:20 for the form). It addresses them in the most insulting terms possible, as children of witches, adulterers, and whores (v 3bc; cf. Isa. 1:4), revealing their character by pointing to the character of their mothers (cf. 1 Sam. 20:30; Ezek. 16:44). They are children of rebellion (v 4de; cf. Isa. 1:2; 48:8), subversive of Yahweh's rule, deliberately opposed to him in defiant sin.

< *5-10* > The case against the scorners is then laid out, and here the words of Isa. 40:1 are echoed. Yahweh there promised to comfort or have compassion on his people, but the false Judeans have sought their comfort from the gods of the Canaanites instead (v 5a). They have worshiped the gods of fertility in the groves ("under every green tree"), in the valley (v 6a), upon the high places (v 7), engaging in sacred prostitution (v 7b, 8d, 8f), sacrificing to false deities, apparently worshiping phallic symbols (v 6a), even practicing the awful rites of child sacrifice (v 5cd), known in earlier times (cf. Jer. 7:31; 19:5; 2 Kings 3:27; 16:3). "Should I comfort them because of these practices?" Yahweh asks in dismay (v 6e).

Yahweh will give a place in his temple to those who truly love him (56:5). But the Judeans have loved the baal gods (v 8f); they have chosen their own place (v 8g). They have pretended to love Yahweh, writing his Word on their doors and doorposts, as commanded in Deut. 6:4-9, but in reality departing totally from him and the comfort and healing which he would bring them (v 8abc). Yahweh had always been the "portion" of Israel (cf. Jer. 10:16; Ps. 16:5; 142:5), the one from whom Israel lived and had its future; but because the faithless Judeans have chosen to worship idols, Yahweh will give them over to their choice: the idols will be their portion. Let them get life from them! That is the initial verdict in the court case.

< *11-13* > The final declaration of Yahweh the judge is set

forth in vv 11e-13e. Yahweh has remained silent about all of these
offenses for a long time, hoping that the people would repent
(v 11cd). But now he utters his judgment on the whole Zadokite
enterprise, which has taken these idolatrous rebels into its cause.
Yahweh had called for faithfulness (56:1), but they all have been
utterly faithless (v 12). They are therefore on their own (v 13a).
Yahweh will not help them, and so it is inevitable that they can
have no lasting good life in the land (cf. Deut. 30:15-20). Instead,
the faithful, the trusting, the obedient will inherit the land and
have permanent place in the temple on Zion (cf. 56:7; Ps. 37:3, 9).

We see here that prophetic viewpoint on which Jesus drew
when he declared, "Blessed are the meek, for they shall inherit
the earth" (Matt. 5:5). Yahweh's comforting and healing Presence, and a good life in this world, cannot be guaranteed simply
by building a temple and going through religious rites. Such salvation is given by God only to those who rely on him, who love
him as their sole helper, and who are therefore obedient to his
commandments.

In setting forth this judgment oracle, Trito-Isaiah further begins
a theme which will continue in later oracles: the identification of
the righteous Levitical-Deuteronomic-Isaianic party with the Suffering Servant of Deutero-Isaiah. The death of the righteous, and
the ignorance of the consequences of that death, in vv 1-2, are
deliberate reflections of Isa. 53:7-9, and of the "righteous one" in
Isa. 53:11. Deutero-Isaiah had named all Israel the "servant" of
Yahweh (cf. Isa. 41:8-9; 43:10; 44:1, 21; 45:4). And yet, paradoxi-
cally, Deutero-Isaiah had also realized that only some in Israel
would remain faithful and would therefore have the mission of
calling the rest of Israel to salvation (Isa. 49:6). It is this faithful
servant-remnant with which the Levitical-prophetic party is identified, and Trito-Isaiah's prophecy to the unfaithful Judeans is
understood as fulfillment of the mission assigned to the servant
in 49:6abc, a mission which will also increasingly include the
concern of 49:6de (cf. 56:6) for all peoples, in the oracles to follow.

Isaiah 57:14-21

14   And it shall be said:
     Prepare, prepare, make clear a way!
          Remove [every] stumbling block from the way of my
               people!
15   For thus says the high and lofty One,
          who dwells in eternity—holy is his name!—
     On high and apart (lit: holy) I dwell,
          but [also] with the contrite (crushed) and low (humble) in
               spirit,
     to give life to the spirit of the lowly,
          and to give life to the heart of the contrite.
16   For not to eternity will I go to court,
          and not forever will I be angry;
     for I clothe a person (lit: spirit) [with flesh],
          and I [alone] make living beings.

          ———

17   With the iniquity of his unjust gain I was angry.
          I smote him and hid myself, because I was angry;
     and he continued backsliding in the way of his heart—
18   I saw his ways!
     But [now] I will heal him and guide him and restore (repay)
          consolations (comfortings) to him,
19   creating for his mourners
          that comfort for which they mourn (lit: fruit of the lips).
     Peace, peace to the far and to the near,
          says Yahweh; and I will heal him.
20   But the wicked will be like the troubled sea,
          unable to rest,
     whose waters stir up mire and mud.
21   There is no peace, says my God, for the wicked.

It is interesting that some commentators who rearrange the
oracles of Trito-Isaiah place this oracle of salvation among the
earliest utterances, because of its similarity to Second Isaiah, while
57:1-13 are placed very late in the sixth century B.C. But the two

oracles are tied inextricably together, a fact recognized by the redactor's addition of the opening phrase in 14a. And both oracles are addressed to the same group—namely, to those in Judah who are followers of the Zadokite priestly party. Yahweh's court sentence of judgment has been pronounced on the idolatrous, even murderous, ways of the Zadokite sympathizers, in 57:1-13. But Yahweh's judgment is never his last Word, not even in the face of the heinous sins detailed in 57:1-13. Nothing and no one stand outside of his mercy. If they did, that would be a stumbling block (57:14) to faith (cf. Isa. 8:14; Jer. 6:21; Ps. 119:165). Indeed, who of us could then be saved? All of us have sinned against God in one way or another. So it is that Yahweh here commands that the stumbling block of judgment also be removed; that the merciful invitation to return once more be extended; that the promise of healing and guidance and comfort once more be made, in the hope that the Judeans—and we—will accept his saving fellowship.

< *14* >   The call goes forth from Yahweh to prepare a way for "*my* people"—sinners can still be his! The language of the verse is very similar to that of Isa. 40:3, but here the way is no longer one on which Yahweh will return to his people, bringing the exiles with him (40:3-11). The way is now a spiritual way on which the Judeans may return to Yahweh. The great heart of mercy is here pleading for repentance (cf. Mark 1:2-3 and pars.; John 1:23).

< *15* >   Yahweh makes this plea on the basis of his self-description in v 15, and of his promises in vv 16-19. He is the "high and lofty One," the absolutely transcendent God (cf. Isa. 6:1), who dwells in heaven (cf. Isa. 33:5; such is the conception also throughout Deut.), far above his creation (cf. Isa. 40:22), unaffected by the transitory nature of time and human life (cf. Isa. 40:6-8, 28; 51:6; Deut. 33:27), utterly different from anything in his creation: such is the meaning of God's "holiness." And yet, this transcen-

dent, holy God deigns to lower himself and to dwell also with
the humble, the meek, the helpless, and all those who have been
crushed and dispirited by the adversities of human life (cf. Ps.
51:17; 34:18; 147:3; Matt. 5:3).

There is a wide range of meaning in the phrase, "contrite and
low in spirit," v 15d. First of all, it refers to all sufferers who have
been battered about by the exigencies of living day by day. And
the overwhelming mercy of God throughout the Bible is that he
sees the affliction of his people, and hears their cry (cf. 1 Sam.
9:16), and knows their sufferings, and comes down to deliver
them out of their bondage to death and evil (cf. Exod. 3:7-8).
Whether that deliverance be the rescue out of Egypt in the Old
Testament, or the deliverance wrought by Christ on the cross and
in the resurrection in the New Testament, God constantly deliv-
ers those who have no other helper. He sides always with the
poor, the oppressed, the sufferer (cf. Luke 1:51-53). He is preju-
diced always for the "crushed," a prejudice mirrored constantly in
Jesus' parables and sayings and actions.

But there is more meaning to "contrite and low in spirit." It
refers also to humility before the holy God, to openness and will-
ingness to accept his saving presence (cf. Matt. 9:12-13). God will
have nothing to do with the proud (cf. Isa. 2:6-22; Ps. 138:6),
with those who think they can make it on their own and who
therefore set about to formulate their own plans and write their
own laws and depend on their own wisdom and strength quite
apart from their Creator (cf. Gen. 3:4-6; 11:4). "Blessed are the
poor in spirit," says Jesus, "for theirs is the kingdom of heaven"
(Matt. 5:3): theirs is the rule of God over their lives; theirs is
the divinely intended relationship of creature with Creator; theirs
is an everlasting fellowship with the sovereign Lord over all
nature and history; and therefore, theirs is a participation in the
victory of that sovereign Lord over all the forces of evil and
destruction and death.

Both of these meanings are included in v 15d, for the Judeans
to whom Yahweh speaks through Trito-Isaiah suffer the external

deprivations of living in a desolate and conquered land. But many of them have also joined cause with the proud—with a Zadokite party that believes it can compel God to find favor with Judah by rebuilding the temple and reinstituting the cult (cf. Hag. 1:1-11; Ezek. 43:1-9). The message of Trito-Isaiah is that Yahweh comes and dwells instead with the humble, with those who cleave to him in heartfelt love and obedient faithfulness and total dependence (cf. v 13). Moreover, when Yahweh comes, he gives to the humble, life (v 15ef)—that abundant life and good for which he alone is the source (cf. Ps. 113:5-9; John 10:10). It is that life which is here offered, in free mercy, even to the opponents of the Levitical-prophetic party.

< 16 >   This offer of life is further reinforced by a promise. In 57:3, Yahweh had taken the sinful idolators to court, and in 57:13, judgment had been pronounced upon them. But here in v 16 the promise is made that Yahweh will not go to court and condemn them forever (cf. 54:8-10; Ps. 103:9; Mic. 7:18). Ours is a Father who has a hard time remaining angry with his children (cf. Hos. 11:8-9; Jer. 31:20). The reason given, in 16cd, is that he has made us (clothed us with flesh, cf. Job 10:11) and has no desire to destroy his handiwork. He tenderly recalls our frailty (cf. Ps. 78: 38-39), and pities us as a father pities his children (Ps. 103:13-14).

< 17 >   His anger was but for a moment (cf. 54:7-8) against the Judeans, because of their oppression of their fellows ("unjust gain," cf. 56:11; Jer. 6:13) and their continual disobedience, born of their faithless hearts (cf. v 11; Jer. 3:14, 22; 31:22; 49:4 all use the same terminology in the Hebrew). None of their faithlessness has been hidden from Yahweh; he has seen their ways (v 17d; cf. 56:11; 57:10, 12).

< 18-19 >   Nevertheless—always the Bible has that stunning reversal of what we deserve—Yahweh will heal Judah (cf. 57:8c; 19:22; 30:26; 53:5; Jer. 3:22) and guide him and repay his faith-

lessness with the comfort originally announced by Second Isaiah (40:1; cf. 57:5, 6). Those who now mourn shall be comforted (v 19): once again we find a passage from which Jesus drew in his beatitudes (Matt. 5:4). Despite all past sin, Yahweh will come to the humble in heart in forgiveness, pronouncing his peace and fullness of life upon them (v 19cd; cf. Isa. 26:12; 32:17), a promise which reminds of nothing so much as Jesus' return to his frightened and faithless disciples, after the resurrection, with his pronouncement, "Peace be with you" (John 20:21; cf. Acts 2:39; Eph. 2:17).

< 20-21 >   Yahweh's offer of mercy to the sinful is not an offer of cheap or automatic grace, however. Many commentators have excised vv 20-21 as later additions to the oracle, but these verses are totally consonant with what has been said in v 15 (cf. 48:22; 3:11; Job 18:5-21). Yahweh will not come to the proud. He will not dwell with those who will not open their hearts to his saving Presence. He will be Lord over us, or he will not be with us and for us at all. And apart from him, there can be no "peace": the word in the Hebrew is *shalom,* which has the meaning of "abundant life." Apart from God, there is only restlessness, and the mire and mud of daily existence.

Isaiah 58:1-14

1   Cry out with all your might! Hold not back!
    Lift up your voice like a ram's horn,
and declare to my people their rebellions,
    and to the house of Jacob their sins!
2   Yet daily they seek me,
    and knowledge of my ways they desire,
as if they were a faithful nation (lit: a nation doing
       righteousness)
    that did not forsake the order (lit: justice) of its God.
They ask of me ordinances of righteousness;
    they desire to draw near to God.

3   [They say to me:] Why do we fast and you do not see?
     [Why] do we afflict ourselves and you do not know?

     ─────────

     Behold! in the day of your fast you seek your own pleasure,
        and all your labors you press.
4   Behold! for strife and contention you fast,
        and in order to hit with your evil fist.
     You do not fast this day
        in order to make your voice heard on high.
5   Is this [the sort of] fast that I choose,
        a day for a man to afflict himself?
     Is it to bow his head like a reed
        and to lie down in the dust in a sackcloth?
     Do you call this a fast
        and a day pleasing (acceptable) to Yahweh?

     ─────────

6   Is this not [rather the sort of] fast I choose:
     To loose the fetters of evil,
        to undo the bands of the yoke,
     To let the crushed (broken) go free,
        and to break every yoke?
7   Is it not to share your bread with the hungry,
        and to bring the cast-out poor into your house;
     when you see someone naked, to cover him,
        and from your own flesh not to hide yourself?
8   Then your light shall break forth like the dawn,
        and your healing (restoration) shall spring up speedily.
     Your salvation (lit: righteousness) will go before you,
        and the glory of Yahweh shall be your rearguard.
9   Then you will call and Yahweh will answer;
        you will cry out, and he will say, "Here am I."

     ─────────

     If you remove from your midst the yoke,
        the pointing of the finger and speaking wickedness,
10   if you give of yourself (lit: cause your self to go forth) to
            the hungry,
        and satisfy the need (lit: self) of the oppressed,

then your light shall rise in the darkness,
and your gloom shall be like the noonday.
11 Then Yahweh will guide you continually,
and in the dry times (places; lit: droughts), he will satisfy
your need.
Your bones he will make strong,
and you will be like a garden soaked [with rain],
like a spring of waters,
whose waters never fail.
12 Then the ancient ruins will be rebuilt by some of you (lit:
from you),
the old foundations you shall raise up.
And you shall be called, "Repairer of the breach,"
"Restorer of ways to rest."

————

13 If you turn back your foot from the sabbath,
[from] doing your [own] pleasure on my holy day,
and [instead], you call the sabbath a delight,
and honor this holy day of Yahweh's—
honor it in all your ways—
not seeking your own pleasure and speaking nonsense
(lit: idly);
14 then you will delight yourself in Yahweh,
and I will make you ride upon the high places of earth;
and I will feed you with the heritage of Jacob your father;
for the mouth of Yahweh has spoken.

The issue has been sharply set forth in the preceding oracles:
the efforts of the Zadokite priestly party to ensure salvation for
Judah—that is, to guarantee Yahweh's presence with her—will
bear no fruit, because such efforts are based on the belief that it
is sufficient simply to rebuild the temple and to restore the cultic
worship. But such external trappings of religion are not automatically efficacious in themselves. They must be accompanied
by the reform of the heart—by turning from the worship of all
other gods to love of Yahweh alone; by the abandonment of one's

own desires and ways to walk only in Yahweh's ways; by the
giving up of proud reliance on one's own devices to depend
humbly and constantly on Yahweh's healing and guidance and
comfort. To all, no matter who they be, who so love and obey and
rely on the transcendent and holy Lord, he will surely come. Such
has been the judgment and the good news announced by Trito-
Isaiah to the followers of the Zadokite party.

In this oracle, Trito-Isaiah now broadens this two-pronged announcement of judgment and salvation to apply it to the activities
of the entire Judean community. The occasion for this oracle is
a day of fasting and lamentation, when the entire community is
engaged in prayers of repentance and pleading, and in the ritual
exercises of wearing sackcloth, bowing down in the dust, marking
their foreheads with ashes, crying out for Yahweh's mercy, and
beating their breasts in gestures of mourning. These were standard practices, carried out whenever the community or an individual faced some crisis (cf. Josh. 7:6; Judg. 20:26; 1 Sam. 7:6;
1 Kings 21:27; Ps. 35:13-14; for the laws of fasts, see Lev. 16:29-
34; 23:27-32; Num. 29:7-11). We do not know what the occasion
was for the particular fast mentioned in Trito-Isaiah. It could
have been that connected with the Day of Atonement (Lev. 16),
or one occasioned by some crisis such as a drought (cf. the emphasis on dryness and water in v 11); but it probably was one of the
four fast days mentioned in Zech. 7:3 and 8:19 that commemo-
rated the siege, capture, and fall of Jerusalem, and the murder of
its governor, Gedaliah. At any rate, Yahweh seizes the opportunity to send his prophets with their message of both judgment
and salvation to the community as a whole, in order to apply
Trito-Isaiah's message also to the ritual practices of lamentation.

< 1 > A prophet is given Yahweh's commission to be a watch-
man for the community, a function indicated by the combination
of the words "cry out" and "ram's horn," i.e., "trumpet" (cf. Isa.
18:3; Jer. 4:5; Ezek. 33:1-9; Hos. 8:1). The commissioned prophet
is to warn Judah that its life is in danger from Yahweh's judg-

ment because of its sins (cf. Mic. 3:8) or rebellions (cf. Isa. 43:27; 56:1) against the King Yahweh. This is a deliberate contrast with the failure of the watchmen in 56:10: the watchmen of the Zadokite party do not fulfill their God-given function, but those of the Levitical party do.

< 2-3b > Yahweh then describes the situation of the people: they are an exceedingly religious people; daily they "seek" him, which means here that they ask the prophets for oracles from Yahweh (cf. Isa. 31:1; Jer. 21:2; 37:7; Ezek. 20:3; Amos 5:4, 6), in order to know how to walk in his ways, according to his ordinances. They say they want to know how to achieve righteousness in Yahweh's eyes, in order that they may enter into fellowship with him—once again "salvation" is defined in terms of Yahweh's presence with them (cf. 56:1). They imagine that if they simply go through the ritual practices of fasting, Yahweh will take notice of them and come to be with them; and they cannot understand why this has not been so (cf. Mal. 3:14). They therefore inquire of the prophets what has gone wrong.

< 3c-5 > A prophet replies, in an indictment of their ways (vv 3c-5), and in instruction (vv 6-7, 9c-10b, 13), and the latter once again shows the prophet exercising his function as an expositor of the torah or teaching of Yahweh (cf. 56:3-8; 1:10-17). Yahweh has not listened to their prayers and taken heed of their plight and come to dwell with them, because they really have not been praying to him and offering true repentance and seeking to walk in his commandments (cf. Isa. 29:13; 48:1; Jer. 7:9-10; Hos. 6:1-6; Zech. 7:5-6; James 4:8; cf. also Jesus' instructions on true fasting, Matt. 6:6-18; 9:14-15). In reality, they have forsaken God (v 2d; cf. 1:4, 28).

Trito-Isaiah spells out the nature of their rebellions in vv 3c-5. The people have been using the fast days to pursue their business as usual: such is the meaning of "seek your own pleasure" in v 3c; they press on with their work, despite the fact that fast days were supposed to be a time of rest (cf. Lev. 16:29, 31; Amos 8:5). The word for "seek pleasure" in v 3c is the same as that for "desire" in v 2b, indicating the contrast between what the people say they want and what they are really seeking (cf. Titus 1:16).

Moreover, the people do not use the fast day for repentance, but for continued oppression of others, v 4. Some commentators imagine that the abstinence from food leads to increased irritability among the Judeans, but it is more likely that the injustices mentioned in 57:1-2, 4, are in the prophet's mind here (cf. Amos 8:4-6).

The outcome, therefore, is that Yahweh takes no notice of their false fasting and repentance. Their voice is not "heard on high," v 4d (cf. Luke 18:9-14). Yahweh does not automatically hear every prayer (cf. Isa. 1:15). Ritual practices such as those mentioned in v 5 do not work in and of themselves, and prayers are not automatically received and answered, and worship does not guarantee the access to God. The persons offering them must first be pleasing and acceptable to the Lord, v 5f (cf. 56:4; 1:10-17; Jer. 7:1-15; Ezek. 8; Hos. 8:11-14; Amos 4:4-5; 5:21-24; Mic. 6:1-8). Such teaching is found throughout the Bible, but seldom heeded by worshipers. If and when we pray, we are certain that God looks kindly on us. Indeed, we sometimes imagine that we are doing him a favor when we worship. We rush carelessly into his house, as if we had a right to be there, and we expect that God will receive us, no matter what the condition of our hearts and lives. The Bible has a different view: we shall be admitted into God's presence only if we are pleasing to him, v 5f; and that raises the fundamental question, How can we be pleasing to him? It is that question over which Trito-Isaiah argues with its Zadokite opponents. It is that question with which much of the New Testament is concerned.

< 6-9b; 9c-12 > In the following strophes, Third Isaiah therefore spells out part of the answer to the question. The fast that Yahweh chooses and the worship that is pleasing to him is the

work (the meaning of "worship" is "service" or "work") of liberation, to remove every yoke that binds human beings to any form of servitude, vv 6, 9c. The prophet is speaking in the most general terms here, and he has in mind not only the oppression of the Levitical-prophetic party, and not only the institution of slavery and the bondage incurred by debt (cf. Amos 2:6-8; Jer. 34:8-9; Neh. 5:10-12). He also speaks of slavery to the gnawing pain of an empty stomach (vv 7a, 10a) and to the misery of homelessness and exclusion from the community (v 7b) and to the shivering shame of being dressed in rags (v 7cd). Those who suffer such bondage wear a yoke of servitude that ultimately crushes their life (the verb is the same as that in the Servant Song, 42:3); and mercy consists in removing their yoke and setting them free (cf. Ezek. 18:7, 16; Job 31:16-20).

The particular acts of kindness mentioned everywhere throughout the Bible are acts which are pleasing to God; the New Testament includes them frequently in its teaching (cf. Matt. 25:34-36; Luke 3:10-11). But the reason given for the acts in v 7d is that we all share a common humanity (so too in Job 31:15). We all are flesh from the hand of God, our one Father. Should we then hide ourselves (i.e., withhold our help; cf. Deut. 22:1, 3, 4) from our own flesh, from our brothers and sisters under God? Once again the viewpoint is universal, encompassing the whole of humankind, and some commentators interpret this passage simply in terms of the humane consideration one human being owes another. But when our Lord gives his reason for such acts of mercy, he goes beyond any merely humanistic views: acts of kindness done to the needy are acts done to him (Matt. 25:45), and he gathers up in his own person all the needy of the world. But he also incarnates in his person the Person of God, and finally an act is good and merciful because God accepts it as such. Humanistic reasoning is replaced with the centrality of the relation to God. The same emphasis is intended here by Trito-Isaiah. This liberation of human beings is good, because God pronounces it good. There is no other standard of good lying outside of his Person.

< *9c-10b* > Probably in these verses the prophet does have the oppression of the Levitical-prophetic party in mind. "Pointing of the finger" (cf. Prov. 6:13) and "speaking wickedness" (cf. Ps. 12:2) refer to the mockery, mentioned earlier in 57:4, directed against the Levitical-prophetic party. We see here that the followers of the Levites and prophets also knew hunger and oppression (c. 57:1-2), a condition experienced often by earlier prophets (cf. 1 Kings 18:3-4; Jer. 20:1-2; 38:6; Isa. 50:6) and finally summed up in that homeless One, who had no place to lay his head (cf. the consequences for the followers of Jesus, 1 Cor. 4:10-13). To minister to their need also was an act pleasing to God (cf. Matt. 10:5-15), and in v 10a, this is framed in terms reminiscent of the openhearted willingness of Deut. 15:7-11 to share oneself and one's goods with the poor.

These are the acts, says Trito-Isaiah, that constitute true fasting in God's eyes, and they are all acts that deny and give up one's self for the sake of others. Without such love for others in need, which at the same time is love for God, self-denial can be nothing more than self-indulgence (cf. 1 Cor. 13:3), a luxuriating in one's own feelings of self-righteousness (cf. Luke 18:12). Or self-denial can be, as here in Trito-Isaiah among the Zadokite party, a futile exercise in magic, designed to coerce the favor of God toward oneself. Ritualism, apart from true love for God and therefore for one's neighbors, will profit nothing. The theology here is very similar to that of Deuteronomy, in which true love for God always issues in mercy toward one's neighbors (cf. Deut. 22:1-4; 24:6, 10-15, 17-22).

Once again, this passage forms the background for two of Jesus' Beatitudes: "Blessed are those who hunger and thirst for righteousness, for they shall be satisfied," and "Blessed are the merciful, for they shall receive mercy" (Matt. 5:6, 7). Up to this point, the teachings of Trito-Isaiah have been very similar to the five opening verses of the Sermon on the Mount, a fact that says much about Jesus' identification with the spirit of the Levitical-prophetic reformers and their role as God's Suffering Servant.

That which is promised to the merciful here in Trito-Isaiah is that their desire to draw near to God (v 2f), to experience the salvation given by his Presence, will indeed become reality (cf. 56:1). The emphasis of vv 8-9b is on that Presence, and Yahweh is described in those verses in four figures:

1) as light, v 8a (cf. 2:5; 9:2; 10:17; 30:26; 51:4, and the reflected light of the Servant, 42:6; 49:6). The verb for "break forth" has the meaning of splitting the heavens; the dawn of Yahweh's Presence will split the heavens, like water bursting forth (cf. 35:6; Gen. 7:11; Ps. 74:15), and will flood the earth with light;

2) Yahweh is compared to "healing," v 8b. In 57:18-19, it was said that Yahweh would heal the people, but here his Presence itself is that healing. To have God with one is to know wholeness (cf. Luke 7:18-23);

3) Yahweh's Presence is described in v 8c as "salvation" (cf. 56:1), and once again his fellowship with the people constitutes the content of salvation;

4) In v 8d, Yahweh is described as the people's "rearguard," the "glory of the Lord" being here a synonym for Yahweh's manifestation of himself on earth (cf. Exod. 33:18-22; Ezek. 1:26-28). Yahweh himself comes to the merciful, and the thought of the strophe is then emphasized in its two closing lines, vv 9a and 9b: the merciful will call to Yahweh (cf. vv 3ab, 4d), and he will answer them (cf. Job 5:1; 14:15); they will cry to him, and he will call out "Here I am!" (cf. 30:19; 55:6), like a father responding to the call of a searching child.

Trito-Isaiah is quoting Isa. 52:12b in v 8c and d, and the way it uses Second Isaiah's words is illustrative of how freely Trito-Isaiah dealt with the traditions of the Isaianic school. Second Isaiah used the words to refer to a new exodus event, namely, the deliverance of the people out of Babylonian exile, borrowing the picture from the original account of the exodus in Exod. 13:21-22; 14:19. Yahweh went before his people, showing them the way; but he was also the "gatherer" behind them, who exhorted the stragglers and gathered them and protected them from the danger that followed (cf. Deut. 25:18). The figure was used of actual deliverance from captivity, originally that from Egypt and then that from Babylonia. Here in Third Isaiah, the language is totally metaphorical; there is no actual "way" on which the people return; they are already in Jerusalem. Instead, the exodus figure is used to symbolize Yahweh's Presence with his people. The renewal of the fellowship with God is the central focus of Trito-Isaiah.

< 9c-12 > The same figures continue to be used in part of the second promissory section, in vv 9c-11. In vv 10c and d, Yahweh is once again the people's "light," which will turn the darkness of their situation into the brightness of noonday (cf. 42:16; Lam. 3:2; Job 11:17; Ps. 37:6). His Presence dispenses every shadow. But the figure of the exodus-leading continues in v 11, and the many references to water in the dry places recall Second Isaiah's pictures of water given in the desert in the new wilderness wandering after the release from Babylonia (Isa. 41:18; 43:19-20; 48:21; 49:10). Once again, however, the figure is metaphorical. Yahweh's Presence will give new vitality to the people (make their bones strong). Yahweh, the spring of living waters (cf. Jer. 2:13; John 4:14), will pour out such abundant life on his people (cf. Isa. 44:3) that their vitality will become like a fountain of waters that never fails (cf. John 7:38).

With such renewed strength given them, the people will be able to rebuild their ancient city (cf. 44:26, 28; 45:13; Ezek. 36:10; Amos 9:11), to repair the breaches in its fallen wall (cf. Ezek. 13:5), and to restore that "rest" (cf. Deut. 3:20; 12:9; Exod. 33:14) from all their "enemies round about" (Deut. 12:10; 25:19; cf. Josh. 11:23) promised to them in the Deuteronomic teaching. Trito-Isaiah has not only Judah's physical restoration in mind. Above all, it proclaims here the promise of Yahweh to restore abundant life to his people.

< 13-14 > Many scholars separate this last strophe from the

oracle, terming it an addition similar to that of 56:1-8 and 66:18-24. But the whole poem is framed by the references to Jacob, vv 1 and 14, and is held together by its contrasts: those who seek their own pleasures (vv 3, 13) are not pleasing to Yahweh (v 5). They must choose what he chooses (v 6). Then they will be able to delight themselves in the Lord (v 14). It does no good to afflict themselves in penance (vv 3, 5) if they are afflicting others (vv 7, 10). If they satisfy others, Yahweh will satisfy them (vv 10, 11).

The word for "sabbath" in v 13 is the same as that used for "rest" in v 12, so that the thought of the sabbath rest follows naturally on the thought of rest in the land, in v 12. The call to honor the sabbath (cf. 56:2, 4, 6) is the same as that to honor the fast day in v 3: in both instances, the Judeans are bidden to cease from pursuing their business as usual and to set aside time for rest, in recognition of Yahweh's lordship over them. (It should be noted that the commandment about the sabbath has to do with rest, not worship). "Speaking nonsense" probably refers to business deals (cf. Hos. 10:4), and the call to honor or magnify Yahweh's lordship in all their ways once again picks up the contrast found in 55:8 between human ways and Yahweh's (see the comment on 56:9-12). But to "honor" Yahweh's holy day is much more than legalistically to follow his commandment for the sabbath. To honor the sabbath is to "delight" in it, v 13c, to find in its period of rest and relaxation that good enjoyment that belongs to life at its best.

If the Judeans delight in the sabbath, then they will find that they will also be able to "delight" themselves in Yahweh, v 14a (cf. Job 22:26)—that is, he will draw near to them and be God to them. In sheer exultation, they will be exalted and will rejoice in the abundant and secure life Yahweh gives: such is the meaning of v 14b (cf. Deut. 32:13; 33:29; Isa. 33:16; Hab. 3:18-19). They will know undisturbed possession of the land, v 14c (cf. 57:13; 1:19). Such is the promise of the God who never takes back his word, v 14d (cf. 40:8; 55:10-11). An oracle that began

with the declaration of Israel's sins, ends with the sure promise
of salvation from God.

The theological question raised by this oracle, however, is
whether or not it involves works-righteousness. The conditional
phrasing of the promise of salvation ("if"-"then," vv 9c-14) seems
to indicate that the Judeans will earn the right, by mercy toward
others and sabbath rest and true fasting, to have Yahweh draw
near to them and dwell with them. Is God's Presence with us
dependent on what we do? The prophet here would seem to be
no less misguided than the Zadokites, who think to coerce Yahweh's favor by restoration of a pure cult. Do our deeds of mercy
compel Yahweh's favor, and the lack of them incur his judgment
upon us? We cannot yet answer this question fully on the basis
of what we have read in the Third Isaiah. Certainly in 57:14-21,
unearned grace was offered to Judah. But in this oracle, grace
seems to be earned. We shall have to keep the question in mind
as we proceed through the following oracles.

Isaiah 59:1-20

1 Behold! Yahweh's hand is not shortened, that it cannot
     save,
     and his ear is not dull, that it cannot hear.
2 But your sins!—
     they are separating you from your God,
     and your iniquities have caused him to hide his face
     from you—from hearing [you].
3 For your hands are stained with blood,
     and your fingers with iniquity.
   Your lips speak a lie;
     your tongue utters wickedness.

———

4 There is no one who goes to law (lit: speaks) justly,
     and there is no one who judges faithfully.
   Relying on chaos (emptiness) and speaking nothingness,
     they conceive mischief and bring forth iniquity.

5   They hatch a viper's eggs,
    and they weave a spider's web.
    Whoever eats their eggs, dies,
       and if one [of the eggs] is broken, a viper crawls (lit:
          breaks) out [of it].
6   Their webs will not be [sufficient] to cover them,
       and they will not [be able to] hide themselves with their
          doings.
    Their doings are deeds of iniquity,
       and a work of violence is in their hands.
7   Their feet run towards evil,
       and they hasten to shed innocent blood.
    Their thoughts are thoughts of iniquity;
       violence and destruction are in their ways.
8   They do not know the way of peace,
       and there is no justice in their paths.
    They make their roads crooked;
       no one traveling them knows peace.

                        ——————

9   Therefore [God's] order (lit: justice) is far from us,
       and salvation (lit: righteousness) does not overtake us.
    We look for light, and behold! darkness;
       for brightness, [but] we walk in the gloom.
10 We grope like blind persons [for a] wall,
       and like those who have no eyes, we feel our way along
          (lit: grope).
    We stumble at noonday as [if] in twilight,
       in the darkness, like the dead.
11 We growl like she-bears, all of us,
       and like doves mourning (lit: moaning), we moan.
    We look for order (lit: justice), and there is none,
       for salvation, [but] it is far from us.
12 For our rebellions are many before you,
       and our sins testify against us;
    for our rebellions are with us,
       and we know our iniquities:
13 rebelling and denying Yahweh,

and turning back (backsliding) from following our God;
committing violence and apostasy,
conceiving and uttering lying words from [our] heart.
14 Therefore order (lit: justice) is turned back,
and salvation stands afar off,
because truth has fallen in the streets,
and equity cannot gain an entrance.
15 Therefore truth is lacking,
and he who departs from evil becomes a prey.

———

But Yahweh saw it and it displeased [him]
that there was none of his order (lit: in his eyes that there
was no justice).
16 And he saw that there was no man,
and he was astonished that there was no one to
intercede.
Therefore he relied on his [own] arm (lit: his arm saved
him),
and he was moved by his own covenant faithfulness
(lit: his righteousness upheld him).
17 Therefore he put on covenant faithfulness
(lit: righteousness) like a breastplate,
and a helmet of salvation on his head;
and he put on a robe of vengeance,
and wrapped himself in a cloak of jealousy (zeal).
18 According to what is deserved, he will repay:
wrath to his adversaries; payment to his enemies;
((to the coastlands a recompense he will repay)).
19 Therefore those in the west shall fear the name of Yahweh,
and those in the east, his glory;
for he will come like a pent-up river,
driven forward by the wind of Yahweh;
20 and he will come to Zion as a redeemer,
to those in Jacob who turn from rebellion.
Oracle of Yahweh.

This judgment-salvation oracle is intimately connected with

ch. 58, because it is built around the form of a communal prayer
of lament, which was uttered during rites of penance and fasting.
Verse 1 directly answers questions voiced often in such laments
about Yahweh's power to save. Verses 9-12 are words taken from,
or at least modeled after, such actual lamenting prayers. And
vv 15c-19 represent the salvation oracle offered by the priest in
answer to the community's lament and petition. Trito-Isaiah is
using well-known forms of liturgical expression here and, in the
manner of all the prophets, is identifying with the community.
The prophets never considered themselves cut off from the community, but were bound up with it in the bundle of life, sharing
its sins and need (cf. Isa. 6:5).

However, at every point Trito-Isaiah goes beyond the standard
liturgical form. The answer given in v 1 is expanded into a
thoroughgoing indictment of the community's life, in the form
of a prophetic torah, vv 2-8. Again and again we see Third Isaiah
exercising this teaching function (cf. Isa. 1:10-17, 18-20). The community's general confession of sin in v 12 is expanded into a chill-
ing catalogue of rebellion in vv 13-15b. A Divine Warrior hymn
is used in vv 15c-19 to announce Yahweh's coming salvation, but
a new twist is given to its meaning, in the closing lines of v 20.
A new situation demands a new interpretation of the Word of
God, and we see in Third Isaiah how traditional forms and
expressions were carried forward, but reinterpreted and altered to
match the moment, a phenomenon continually exhibited throughout the Scriptures (cf. the reinterpretations given to Mark by
Matthew and Luke). The Word of God is never a dead letter
from the past, but always a living, restless, demanding force
affecting the present.

The oracle is directed to the Judean community as a whole,
which has followed the lead of the Zadokite priestly party, but
which finds that its cries to Yahweh go unheard, that its worship
is received by no one, and that Yahweh does not come to be with
it or give it his abundant life.

< *9-11* > The community's situation is vividly pictured in its
words of lament. Yahweh's order and salvation remain distant
from them, v 9ab (cf. 58:3). The words are literally "justice" and
"righteousness" in the Hebrew (cf. 56:1), but justice *(mishpat)*
is, as in Second Isaiah, that order which Yahweh's power bestows
on human society in contrast to chaos (cf. v 4c; 42:1, 3, 4; 45:18-
19); and righteousness *(tzedeqah)* is, again as in Second Isaiah,
synonymous with the salvation and abundant life which Yahweh's Presence brings to his people (cf. 51:5). Further, throughout the Bible, chaos is associated with evil, darkness, death (cf.
Gen. 1:2-3; Rev. 21:1-4, 22-25), while Yahweh's Presence and salvation are associated with light (cf. 58:8, 10; 51:4; John 1:4-5;
Rev. 22:5). Therefore Yahweh's absence from the community
is compared to darkness (cf. 8:22; 50:10-11), and apart from
Yahweh, life—so frequently described in the Old Testament as
a walk upon a way—is likened to the groping stumbling of the
blind (cf. 56:10; 42:7, 16, 18-19; 8:14-15; 28:13; 6:9-10; Lam. 4:14,
17; Matt. 15:14; 23:16, 24; John 11:9-10; Rom. 2:19), a situation
that Deuteronomy considered inevitable for those deserting the
Lord (Deut. 28:29). Noonday (cf. 58:10) becomes like twilight
(cf. Job 5:14; Jer. 13:16; Amos 5:18, 20), and the Judeans dwell
in a gloom comparable to that in Sheol, the place of the dead (cf.
57:9; Lam. 3:6). The growling like bears is an unusual figure
(cf. Isa. 5:30), while the cooing of the dove was considered a
mourning sound (cf. Isa. 38:14; Ezek. 7:16; Nah. 2:7). Both may
refer to the sounds made by the lifeless shades in Sheol who,
according to Isa. 8:19, merely "chirp and mutter"; gone is the
praise of Yahweh appropriate to those who are alive (cf. Ps.
115:17). In their own eyes, and those of the prophet, the Judeans
are as good as dead.

< *12* > In the confession of this verse, the Judeans acknowledge
the reason for their situation: they have sinned against Yahweh
and, as in a court of law, their sins bear testimony against them
(cf. 3:9; Jer. 14:7—also a communal lament; Hos. 5:5). They

know they have done evil (cf. Ps. 51:3; 90:8). Indeed, they do not hesitate to use the strongest term to describe their sin: "rebellion" against Yahweh (cf. 58:1). But they mention no specific acts of wrongdoing, and the confession is very general, much like the prayers of confession we repeat in our churches on Sunday morning.

< 13-15b > One of the characteristics of the Bible, however, is that it always gets down to specifics. The relation with God cannot be lived out in general, but only in the most specific terms of obedience and trust, or of rebellion and lack of loving dependence on God. As our salvation is spelled out in the most concrete acts by God, so our sin is also manifested in the most specific deeds and failures on our part, and in the expansion added to the communal confession, in vv 13-15b, as well as in the indictment of vv 3-8, Trito-Isaiah gets down to specifics.

< 1-2 > First, however, Trito-Isaiah answers the lament of the community. Yahweh has not closed his ears to his people (cf. 58:4; 1:15; Ezek. 8:18), and hidden his face from them (cf. 57:17; 8:17; Job 34:29), and refused to come to them because he can not or will not give them abundant life. Rather, the people's sins have created a great gulf between them and their God. It is the Judeans who have separated themselves from God, not God who has distanced himself from them. And the thought is emphasized by the personal terms with which Yahweh is described in the oracle. He has hands, ears, a face, vv 1-2, and in vv 15c-20, he has arms, a name, breath. He clothes himself like a warrior there, with armor and helmet and cloak.

The Old Testament uses such anthropomorphisms because it always emphasizes the personal nature of God. This deity wishes to dwell with his people in the personal relationship of love and trust and faithfulness. This God yearns for his people and weeps over them and seeks them like a loving parent. Only our sin could possibly keep him from our side. Only our rejection of his love could possibly keep him from being with us. We turn and walk away from him; that is the cause of the separation: love rejected, compassion refused, life disdained in favor of death. Such is the incredible nature of our sin against our God.

< 3-8 > The prophet then details in these verses the specifics of the Judeans' sin. Their hands are stained with blood, v 3a (cf. 57:1-2; 1:15, 21; Jer. 2:34), that is, they have caused the death of the innocent, as also in v 7b, and the whole of vv 3-4 probably refer to corrupt practices in the court of law. "You shall not bear false witness against your neighbor" was the stipulation in the Decalogue (Exod. 20:16; Deut. 5:20), but they have lied about their neighbors (cf. 57:4d; 11b; 28:15e; 30:9; Pss. 12; 101:5, 7; 109:1-5; 120), accusing them falsely (cf. Jer. 9:4-9) and bringing unjust sentences and sometimes even death upon them. Moreover, the practice is widespread: no one goes to court justly (cf. 10:1-2; 29:21; Jer. 5:28; Amos 5:10-13, and the elders who gather in the city gates to hear cases never judge the case rightly. The reason for the corruption, however, is that the Judeans are allied with the forces of death and with the great void of chaos (v 4c; cf. 28:14-18; 30:12; Ezek. 13:8; Zech. 10:2). They are pregnant with mischief or trouble and therefore able to bring forth only iniquity, v 4d (cf. 33:11; Job 15:35; Ps. 7:14). Here the prophet is referring to the Judeans' reliance on the Zadokite priestly party.

Verses 5-8 specifically describe the deeds of that party. Many scholars have considered these verses to be secondary, because they could not identify those being described. But it is clear that Trito-Isaiah sees the Zadokite party as the source of evil in the community, and the description given of the Zadokite leaders is devastating. Their plans hatch evil ("a viper's eggs," cf. 14:29), and their projects to restore the community are as fragile and impermanent as a spider's web (cf. Job 8:14). Those who follow their plans ("whoever eats their eggs") will inherit not life but death (in contrast to Yahweh's promise in 58:14). That which breaks forth (the same verb as in 58:8) from their projects is not light but darkness, not sustenance but poison (cf. Deut. 32:33).

However, as in 57:12 and 18a, Yahweh knows their deeds, and they cannot hide their true nature behind false piety, v 6ab (cf. 28:20). Their doings are really deeds of iniquity and violence (cf. Jer. 6:7; Ezek. 7:23). Indeed, they *run* to do evil and to corrupt justice (cf. 57:1-2; Prov. 1:16; 6:18). There is no rejoicing in what is good and true and right (cf. 1 Cor. 13:6), no hungering and thirsting for righteousness, no eager seeking after the ways of God's order for the human community. Their thoughts are not centered on God's ways, but on their own desires, and so they can only bring forth iniquity, violence, destruction, v 7 (cf. Rom. 3:10-18). Apart from God they cannot know the way to abundant life ("peace," cf. 57:19, 21; Jer. 8:15; 14:19; Luke 1:79; 19:42) and to the order of God's justice (cf. 56:1; 58:2). Their ways become crooked (cf. Prov. 2:15; 10:9; 28:18), twisting, torturous passages through an existence that can never know Yahweh's good, v 8 (cf. Ps. 1). As throughout Third Isaiah, life is a walk on a way (cf. 56:11; 57:10, 14, 18), and the repetition of the verb for not knowing emphasizes that the Zadokite leaders and their followers have missed the proper way.

We see here the interior nature of biblical faith. As in Jesus' teaching in Mark 7:14-23, it is not outward deeds of piety that determine the character of a person's life (cf. also 1 Cor. 13:13), but the inner focus of the heart and mind. If one's whole desire is to follow after God and his commandments for life, then needs of goodness issue naturally (cf. Phil. 4:8-9), and the outward actions and their result, in turn, strengthen the inner resolve. Obedience becomes a further confirmation of faith. But if the heart and mind are not centered on God in the first place, and do not hunger and thirst after his guidance and lordship over life, then true goodness is impossible and obedience to God's commands becomes a burdensome legalism (cf. Gal. 5:16-24). Everything in the devout life hangs on that love of the heart, and it is in their inner selves,

Trito-Isaiah maintains, that the Zadokite party has rejected fellowship with God.

< *13-15b* > The nature of this rejection is summarized, then,
in these verses that are an addition to the communal lament of
vv 9-12. Verse 13 puts in four participial phrases everything that
the passage has said previously about the Judeans' sin. Verses 14
and 15a summarize the result of that sin: Yahweh's order and
salvation for the community remain afar (cf. 1:21-23; Hab. 1:4).
Verse 15b repeats what was said in 57:1-2: those who reject the
Zadokite party's leadership and who try to follow after Yahweh
are subjected to persecution and even death.

In short, Trito-Isaiah makes it very clear that what Yahweh
does toward us is fundamentally affected by what we do toward
him (cf. Matt. 10:32-33). God takes sin seriously. It cannot be hid
behind an outward show of piety and worship. He will not give
his abundant life to those who deny him and rebel against him,
to those who do not yearn for him in their hearts and who do
not hunger to follow his commandments. He will not come to be
with those who have no use for him, and thus the salvation accompanying his Presence will remain unknown and unexperienced
by all who do not love him. And that is a situation glibly accepted
by our generation. Who needs God anyway? we ask. Life is very
good as it is: our stomachs are full; our houses are sound; our
bodies are clothed in the latest fashion. We can participate in the
enjoyment of our technological culture with gusto and even aban-
don. Who needs God, we think, when life is so full and satisfying?

< *15b-20* > The final section of this oracle reveals, however, that
God does not passively accept such rejection of him. His lordship
over his creation is never dispelled or defeated by our denial of
that lordship. Yahweh comes. Whether we want him to or not,
he comes to set up his kingdom and to establish his rule over the
earth. The question with which we are confronted finally is, How
will we stand in the day of his coming? As Jesus framed it,

"When the Son of man comes, will he find faith on earth?"
(Luke 18:8).

Trito-Isaiah announces this coming of Yahweh, vv 15c-20, by
employing the ancient motif of Yahweh the Divine Warrior.
From the time of the exodus on, Israel often described her God in
the symbols of a Man of War. Yahweh was the all-powerful conqueror who put down Israel's enemies and brought salvation to
his peoples (cf. Exod. 15:1-18, esp. v 3; Deut. 33:2-5, 26-29; Judg.
5:4-5; Ps. 68; Hab. 3:2-15, etc.). In the prophecies of Jeremiah and
Ezekiel, however, it was announced that Yahweh had turned to
fight against his own people because of their sin (cf. Jer. 4:19-22,
5-8, 29-31; 5:15-17; 6:1-5, 6-8, etc.; Ezek. 7; 13:5; see also Lam.
2:5; 3:2, 43). The opening good news of forgiveness in the prophecies of Second Isaiah therefore announced that this warfare of
Yahweh against his people was finally ended (40:2), and that
prophet pictured Yahweh as a mighty Warrior once again rescu-
ing his people from their enemies and from exile (42:13; 52:10).

So here too in Trito-Isaiah, Yahweh arms himself to bring salvation to his people and judgment on his enemies. But there is
a new twist: now the enemies are within not without the community of Israel, namely the unfaithful Judeans. Both Yahweh's
judgment and his salvation are to be exercised first of all within
the borders of Judah itself. The oracle is intended therefore as a
warning to the unfaithful to turn from their rebellion against
God before it is too late, and to participate in the redemption
that Yahweh will bring to the faithful, v 20 (cf. Ezek. 18:30-32;
Rom. 11:26-27).

The beginning lines of the Divine Warrior section, vv 15c-16,
emphasize that the establishment of Yahweh's order and abundant life in the community will be solely his act (cf. Exod. 14:13-
14). There is no one else (cf. 41:28; 50:2; 57:1) who can bring
salvation—especially not the Zadokites who think to coerce Yahweh by their ritual. But Yahweh is astonished that no prophetic
intercessors have been pleading with him for the life of the community, v 16b (cf. Ezek. 22:30). However, his own arm has all

power to save (cf. v 1; 40:10; 48:14; 51:5, 9; 52:10; Ps. 98:1), and his faithfulness to his covenant with his people motivates him to act on their behalf. He clothes himself in his military garb (cf. Eph. 6:14, 17; 1 Thess. 5:8) and wraps himself in a cloak of jealousy, v 17.

Yahweh is a jealous God. That affirmation is made throughout the Old Testament (cf. Exod. 20:5; 34:14; Deut. 5:9; Zech. 8:2), but we are not to picture him as some sort of green-eyed monster. Yahweh's jealousy is his zeal (the word is the same in the Hebrew)—his zeal for his purpose of love (cf. Isa. 9:7) in which he has enlisted Israel. He desires to bring his blessing on all the families of the earth (Gen. 12:3), and he has chosen Israel with a special love (cf. Deut. 7:6-8) to be his instrument in the realization of that goal. He is the Lord, working out his plan for all of history, and nothing will deter him from the fulfillment of that plan. He is jealous for it; he is zealous for its realization; and thus too he is jealous for Israel, his beloved servant-people, whom he will let no one else claim or destroy, and who are to love no other god but him. Thus, in v 17d, Yahweh comes in his jealous zeal to continue the implementation of his purpose in human history.

Part of that implementation is the defeat of his enemies, v 18ab —v 18c is a gloss—(cf. Job 34:11; Isa. 35:4; Jer. 17:10). If Yahweh is the Lord, then those who oppose his lordship must be destroyed before Yahweh can establish his good kingdom on earth. His enemies will receive the just reward of their rebellion against him (cf. Gal. 6:7-10): that is the fearful part of the announcement of God's coming. And the power with which God comes in retribution is vividly pictured in the figure of v 19cd: Yahweh bursts onto the human scene like a great wall of water, initially dammed up, but now released and driven forward by the mighty wind of Yahweh's zealous wrath. All peoples will witness his coming, in a universal theophany (cf. 40:5; 24:14-15), and all will immediately acknowledge that he alone is God (c. 45:6, 14, 24-25), v 19ab. Yahweh's coming to Judah in judgment serves to establish his lordship over the lives of all the inhabitants of earth.

Clearly, how we stand in the day of the coming of the Lord is not a matter of indifference. There is no neutral ground in the relationship with God. Either we are for him in the inner recesses and hungers of our hearts, or we are against him. And when he comes, he will destroy those who are against him. It is this understanding that all of human life is lived out against the backdrop of the final divine assize which we have almost totally lost in our modern society. But our having lost sight of the fact makes it no less true, and Trito-Isaiah serves to remind us of that final decision toward which we journey (cf. Matt. 25:31-46). Yahweh comes as Redeemer (cf. 41:14; 43:1, 14; 44:6, 22, 23, 24, etc.) to those who turn from rebellion—but only to those who turn. To the unrepentant he comes as a jealous and avenging Warrior. To quote Paul's words, "Do not be deceived; God is not mocked, for whatever a man sows, that he will also reap (Gal. 6:7).

Isaiah 59:21

21   And as for me, this is my covenant with them, says Yahweh: my spirit which is upon you and my words which I put in your mouth, shall not depart out of your mouth and out of the mouth of your children's children, says Yahweh, from now and for evermore.

All scholars agree that this verse does not belong with 59:1-20. Some omit it altogether. Westermann inserts it between 66:20 and 22. Others view it as a late addition. But as Trito-Isaiah has been assembled by the Levitical-prophetic community, this verse forms the conclusion to the first part of the book. The book has three major sections: chs. 56-59; chs. 60-62; chs. 63-66. This is the promissory conclusion to the first section.

Yahweh here makes a new covenant with his people (cf. Jer. 31:31-34; Ezek. 36:26-28), that is, he enters into a new relationship with them. But the relationship is vastly different than that promised in Jeremiah or Ezekiel. The new covenant here is that two-pronged relationship set forth in the prophets' words (cf. Jer. 1:9; Isa. 49:2; 51:16), as they have been inspired by the Spirit: judgment to the enemies of Yahweh, salvation to those who love him. This verse is the promise that the oracles of chs. 56-59 will come to pass. The Word of God will not return to him void (cf. 40:8; 55:10-11). The section ends on the same note with which it began (see on 56:1).

Further, that two-pronged message will endure forever in Israel. It will be handed down from one generation to the next. The reference in the final sentence is not to a hereditary continuation of the prophetic gift—prophecy finally died out in postexilic Israel (cf. Zech. 13:2-6)—but to the perpetual remembrance of the prophets' words. And indeed, their words have been handed down and reread and pondered from the time when they were first uttered in the sixth century B.C. until this very day. We have to ask ourselves, therefore, if this relation of both judgment and salvation is the one which God still has with us in Jesus Christ.

Unfolding the Message
PART II Isaiah 60-62

Isaiah 60:1-22

1 Arise! Shine! for your light has come,
  and the glory of Yahweh has risen (shines) upon you.
2 For behold! darkness covers the earth,
  and thick darkness the peoples;
  but upon you Yahweh shines (rises),
  and his glory is seen upon you.
3 And nations shall walk toward your light,
  and kings toward the brightness of your shining.

———

4 Lift up your eyes round about and see!
  They all gather together; they come to you.
  Your sons shall come from afar,
  and your daughters will be carried on the hip (lit: arm).
5 Then you shall see and be radiant,
  and your heart will throb and swell with joy;
  for the abundance of the sea will be turned over to you;
  the wealth of the nations shall come to you.

———

6   A multitude of camels shall cover you,
    young male camels from Midian and Ephah.
They shall all come from Sheba.
    Gold and frankincense they will bring,
and they will announce the praise of Yahweh.
7   All the flocks of Kedar shall be gathered to you;
    rams of the Nabateans shall be at your service
        (lit: shall serve you).
They will ascend [with my favor] to my altar,
    and the house of my splendor I will glorify
        (lit: cause to shine).

---

8   Who are these that fly like a cloud,
    and like doves to their windows?
9   For me (lit: Because to me) the ships are gathering,
    with (lit: and) ships of Tarshish in the lead,
to bring your sons from afar,
    their silver and gold with them,
for the name of Yahweh your God,
    and for the Holy One of Israel, for he will glorify you.

---

10   And foreigners shall build your walls,
    and their kings shall serve you.
For in my wrath I smote you,
    but in my favor I will have compassion on you.
11   And your gates shall be open continually.
    By day and night they shall not be shut,
that the wealth of nations may come to you,
    and their kings led [captive].
12   For the nation and the king which does not serve you
        shall perish,
    and [their] people shall be utterly destroyed.

---

13   The glory of Lebanon shall come to you—
    cyprus, plane, and cedar together—
to beautify (glorify) the place of my sanctuary,
    and the place of my feet I will glorify.

14 And they shall come to you, bowing down,
      the sons of those who oppressed you,
            ((and they shall bow down, bending at your feet,
            all those who despised you,))
      And they shall call you, "City of Yahweh,
      Zion [of the] Holy [One of] Israel."

15 Instead of your being a deserted place,
      hated, with no one passing through,
   I will make you majestic (glorious) forever,
      a joy from generation to generation.
16 And you shall suck the milk of the nations,
      and the breast of kings shall you suck.
   And you shall know that I,
      Yahweh, am your Savior
      and your Redeemer, the Mighty One of Jacob.

17 Instead of bronze
      I will bring gold;
      and instead of iron
      I will bring silver;
   and instead of wood, bronze,
      and instead of stone, iron.
   And I will make your overseers peace
      and your taskmasters salvation (lit: righteousness).
18 And violence shall not be heard again
      in your land,
      oppression and destruction within your borders.
   And you shall call your walls salvation,
      and your gates praise.

19 The sun shall never again be [necessary] to you
      as a light by day;
   and the brightness of the moon
      shall not be [necessary] to give light to you,
   because (lit: but) Yahweh shall be to you
      for light forever,
   and your God for your splendor.

20   Your sun will never set again,
        and your moon will not withdraw,
     for Yahweh will be to you
        for light forever,
     and your days of mourning will be ended.

---

21   And your people—all of them!—shall be saved
          (lit: righteous);
       forever they shall possess the land.
     [They will be] a shoot of Yahweh's (lit: his) planting,
        the work of his hands, to glorify himself.
22   The small shall become as a thousand (tribe),
       and the lowly a powerful nation.
     I! Yahweh! In its time I will hasten it.

After the mixture of conditional promises, scathing judgments, warnings, and calls to repentance of chapters 56-59, we find in the second section of Trito-Isaiah (chapters 60-62) nothing but unconditional, soaring, lyrical proclamations of salvation to the inhabitants of Judah and Jerusalem. The contrast between the two sections seems so jarring that many scholars have concluded that 60-62 cannot possibly be from the same hand as 56-59.

Moreover, 60-62 are more nearly like the oracles of Second Isaiah than are any other portions of Third Isaiah. Time and again the authors of 60-62 borrow quotations, theological motifs, and allusions from chapters 40-55. For example, in chapter 60, 60:4ab = 49:18ab; 60:4c = 49:12a; 60:4d = 49:22e. 60:14 is a variation on 49:23a. 60:9ef parallels 49:26cd and 55:5cd; 60:16cde is like 49:26cde. The thought of 60:1 is like that of 52:2; of 60:5d like 45:14a-d; of 60:10cd like 54:8. The trees listed in 60:13b are listed in 41:19cd. The phrase "oppression and destruction" in 60:18c is found in 51:19c. Israel is called the work of Yahweh's hands in both 60:21d and 45:11d, etc. It is clear that Trito-Isaiah is appropriating the message of Second Isaiah, and reformulating it for its own situation.

In addition, there are many usages in chapter 60 similar to those of First Isaiah, and the influence of the Isaianic school as a whole is strong, while parallels to the Jeremianic-Deuteronomic-Levitical material seem not so prominent. Could chapters 60-62 be the original nucleus of Trito-Isaiah, around which the rest of the book was formed? Many scholars think so, and many would attribute only 60-62 to the prophet himself, with perhaps the addition of the independent oracles of 57:14-20; 65:16b-25; 66:6-16 and 58:1-12 (so Westermann).

As I stated in the introduction, however, Trito-Isaiah is a communal expression, growing out of the Isaianic and Jeremianic-Deuteronomic-Levitical schools, and one cannot isolate an individual prophetic author of it from the community of which he was a part. The book uses many differing traditions from the two prophetic schools from which it stems, and it is only natural in a section such as 60-62, which announces future salvation, that the materials should exhibit parallels primarily to Second Isaiah, for that prophet was, above all others, the great herald of a future salvation.

Why, however, did Trito-Isaiah couple this announcement of unconditional salvation with the conditional announcements in chapters 56-59? How could one and the same prophetic group proclaim in 60:21, "And your people—all of them—shall be saved!" when earlier they had warned, "There is no peace, says my God, for the wicked" (57:21). How could Zion as a whole be told, "And you shall know that I, Yahweh, am your Savior, and your Redeemer, the Mighty One of Jacob" (60:16), when in the immediately preceding oracle she had been warned that Yahweh would come as Redeemer only to those in Zion who turned from their rebellion (59:20)?

The answer is that Trito-Isaiah becomes, in chapters 60-62, representative of the pastoral mercy of God. The call for repentance and the warning of the consequences of disobedience have been issued in chapters 56-59. Especially was the call to repentance set forth in 57:14—59:20. But repentance on the part of sinners cannot be motivated simply by the fear of judgment. No child ever learned true obedience only by being warned of punishment. It is not judgment that furnishes the motive power for faithful living, but mercy. It is not fear that prompts obedient service to God, but love for him. "We love because he first loved us." We give our hearts to God, because we see with what open-hearted mercy he has dealt with us.

And here in chapters 60-62, God offers his open-hearted mercy. He holds out to all the idolators, all the proudly defiant, all the unjust rebels in Zion, his prevenient grace, which takes the initiative in giving them abundant life, even if they do not deserve it. All of you can be saved, he says; all of you can possess the land; all of you can be the little shoot of the vine which I, your Creator and Gardener, will once again plant on my holy mountain. I will keep my promise to your father Abraham. I will multiply you like the stars of the heavens (60:22). All of your fortunes will be reversed, and you shall know life in its fullness. For a little while, I was angry with you, but now I will have compassion on you all (60:10; cf. 57:17-18). Such is the future which this oracle holds out, on behalf of Yahweh, to his remnant people in Judah. It is this future, then, that Trito-Isaiah expects will finally motivate Judah to be faithful—a future that is actually a picture of the coming of the kingdom of God.

The kingdom comes! Unearned, it comes. We see here the biblical view of the relationship between ethics and eschatology (= knowledge of the end). Judah is to be faithful not in order that the kingdom may come, but because it is in fact coming. Judah is to be obedient not out of fear before the judgment which comes with the kingdom, but out of love for the merciful God who will in fact give to the people the kingdom's abundant life. We have begun to deal with the questions about works-righteousness which we raised at the end of the exposition of 58:1-14, and it is this central promissory section on salvation in chapters 60-62 that prevents any legalistic and deadening interpretation of the book. It was absolutely necessary for the community that shaped the book to assemble it as they did, in order to convey the hopeful message of mercy which they had received from the Lord.

< *1-3* > If we ask about the nature of the coming kingdom, in Trito-Isaiah's view, it is quite clear here in chapter 60 that salvation involves the presence of Yahweh with his people—the meaning of salvation which we also saw in the earlier oracles. And Yahweh's presence is overwhelmingly pictured here under the figure of light (cf. 58:8, 10; Col. 1:13). In this case therefore, Yahweh's "glory" in vv 1-2 is his shining effulgence, the material manifestation of his Being of Light upon earth (cf. 35:2; 40:5; 58:8; 59:19; Ezek. 1:26-28; James 1:17; 1 Tim. 6:16). It can therefore be said in vv 19 and 20, that when Yahweh comes to his people they will have no need of sun or moon to give them light, because Yahweh's Presence of Light will be with them. (cf. Isa. 24:23; 2:5; 9:2; Rev. 21:23; 22:5). The people then will shine with a reflected light from Yahweh's glory, vv 2c-3b, just as Moses' face shone when he descended from talking to God on Mt. Sinai (Exod. 34:29; 2 Cor. 3:12-18) and just as we reflect "the light of the knowledge of the glory of God in the face of Christ" (2 Cor. 4:6; cf. Matt. 5:14-15). To this reflected light, all the nations, who now dwell in darkness, will be automatically drawn (vv 2-3), to participate in the worship of Yahweh in his rebuilt temple. It is a picture of a future of cosmic and universal dimensions.

To sense the force with which the picture is presented, the reader should note the constant repetition of two sets of terms. First, there are those depicting light and shining and glory and splendor:

- light, *'or*—vv 1a, 3a, 19b, 19f, 20d; as a verb—19d
- to shine, to be risen, *zrh*—vv 1b, 2c, 3b
- brightness, shining, *ngh*—v 3b
- to be radiant, to shine, *nhr*—v 5a
- splendor, glory, *tph'rh*—vv 7d, 19g
- to glorify, to shine, to beautify, *p'r*—vv 7d, 9f, 13c, 21d

- glory, *kbhdh*—vv 1b, 2d, 13a; as a verb, to honor, to glorify—
  v 13d
- majestic, glorious, *g'n*—v 15c

Second, there is the forceful repetition of

- "come" (vv 4b, 4c, 5d, 6c, 11c, 13a, 14a)
- "gather together" (vv 4b, 7a, 9a)
- "bring" (vv 6d, 9c, 17b, 17d).

The poem is full of the sense of light and of movement, spoken to a people who think there is no light and who feel themselves at a dead end. Yahweh's coming to them will reverse all their fortunes.

< *4-9, 13-14* > It is this reversal of fortune, moreover, which the prophets wish their people to trust and expect, and they use all sorts of figures of speech to inspire that faithful expectation. Jerusalem is addressed in v 1, as a woman, mourning in the dust (cf. 52:2), and she is bidden to get up and to lift up her eyes, v 4. If she does so, she will see the whole world coming to her, because of the glory of Yahweh's saving Presence reflected in her. Like a mother rejoicing over the return of her lost and scattered children, her heart will swell with joy, because the nations will bring those children still in exile back to her, vv 4cd—the sons walking, v 4c, or coming on the ships of the seafarers, v 9c, the infant daughters borne on the hip in the oriental fashion, v 4d (cf. 43:5-6; 11:11-12).

As in the thought of Second Isaiah, the poem implies that when Yahweh saves Israel, the nations will realize that he alone is God, v 14 (cf. 45:14-17, 22-25; 49:7; 52:13—53:12; Zech. 14:16-17). Therefore when they stream to Zion (cf. Isa. 2:2-4), they will not come empty-handed. Rather, they shall bring their treasures with them to be used in rebuilding the temple (vv. 5c, 6d, 7d, 9d, 13a-d; cf. Hag. 2:7-9), and their animals to be offered as sacrifices upon

Yahweh's altar (vv 6ab, 7; cf. 56:7). There will be caravans of
camels bearing gifts from the southwest desert tribes of Midian
and Ephah; gold and frankincense from the Arabian trading
center of Sheba; herds from Kedar and Nabaioth, famous for their
sheep and rams; silver and gold from the sea peoples; fine tim-
ber from the North. All will be used to pay homage to Yahweh
(vv 6e, 9; cf. 42:10-12; 19:19-24). As in the Psalms (99:5; 132:7),
the temple is portrayed in v 13d as the footstool of God (cf. Lam.
2:1; 1 Chron. 28:2). Verse 7c even implies that the sacrificial animals will go up to the altar voluntarily.

< 10-12 > The security and peace which Jerusalem will enjoy
are pictured in the figures of these verses. Jerusalem will have no
need to close its gates as protection from enemies (cf. 54:14-17;
Rev. 21:25-26). Indeed, former enemies will become servants (cf.
41:11-12; 51:22-23; 14:1-2), and those who do not minister to
Jerusalem will be taken captive (v 11d; cf. Isa. 24:21-22; Ps.
149:8) and destroyed. The figure is intended not as an expression
of vengeance (most of v 14b is a gloss), but as still another portrayal of the total transformation of Israel's life.

< 15-17 > Verse 15 very clearly points out that Jerusalem will
become a joy, a place no longer deserted and shunned by other
peoples (cf. Jer. 30:17). Just as it was promised to Abraham by
Yahweh that Israel would be a blessing in the midst of the earth
(Gen. 12:3; cf. Isa. 19:24), so Trito-Isaiah here envisions the fulfillment of that promise. Jerusalem's relation to the world is one
of light shining in the darkness, and the salvation of Israel finally
means, for Trito-Isaiah, the salvation of all peoples. The view remains as broad and open as it was in 56:1-8.

< 18 > Finally, in the figures of this verse, the reversal of Jeru-
salem's internal fortunes is set forth. No longer will there be violence and destruction and oppression in the land, so condemned
in the preceding oracles. Instead, Zion will be ringed by salvation,

like walls enclosing its life (cf. Zech. 2:5), and all who enter will
enter by the gates of the praise of God.

< 21-22 > All this will come about, the oracle promises, because
Yahweh will do it. In his good time (v 22c), Israel's Savior and
Redeemer, the Mighty One of Jacob (v 16; the latter title stems
from the tribal federation of the North), will establish fullness of
life ("peace," v 17f) and salvation (v 17g) in Jerusalem and
Judah. The few, the poor, the oppressed will become the many
and powerful v 22. Yahweh will bring his plan for his kingdom
on earth to fruition in their time. Trito-Isaiah bids his people
trust that promise and live lives obediently expectant of it.

Isaiah 61:1-11

1 The spirit of the Lord Yahweh is upon me,
    because Yahweh has anointed me.
  He has sent me to bring good tidings to the poor;
    to bind up the broken of heart;
  to proclaim to captives, freedom,
    and to those who are bound, loosening;
2 to proclaim a year of favor from Yahweh,
    and a day of vengeance from our God;
  to comfort all who mourn,
3   ((to grant to those who mourn in Zion)),
    to give them a turban instead of dust,
  oil of joy instead of a mourning veil,
    praise instead of a faint spirit;
  and to name them:
      "oaks of salvation (lit: righteousness),
        the planting of Yahweh, that he may glorify himself."

———

4 And they shall build up ancient ruins;
    devastations of old they shall raise up.
  And they shall restore desolate cities,
    devastations from past generations
      (lit: generation to generation).

5 And aliens shall stand
   and feed your sheep,
      and foreigners shall be your plowmen and
      your vine-dressers.
6 But you! "priests
   of Yahweh" you shall be called;
      "ministers of our God,"
      it shall be said to you;
   the wealth of nations you shall eat,
      and with their abundance you shall be transformed
      (lit: you shall change places).

---

7 Instead of their two-fold shame
   and reproach, they shall rejoice in their portion.
   Because they will have double possession in their land;
      joy everlasting shall be theirs.
8 For I, Yahweh—
      lover of justice,
         hater of robbery with burnt offering—
   I will faithfully give their reward,
      and I will make an everlasting covenant with them.
9 And their descendants shall be renowned among the
            nations,
      and their offspring in the midst of the peoples.
   All who see them shall acknowledge
      that they are a seed whom Yahweh blesses.

---

10 I will rejoice greatly in Yahweh;
       my [whole] self will exult in my God,
    for he has clothed me in garments of salvation,
       [with] a robe of deliverance (lit: righteousness) he has
          covered me,
    like a bridegroom who adorns himself with a turban,
       and like a bride who decks herself in a bridal garment.
11 For as the earth brings forth its vegetation,
       and as a garden causes its seeds to grow,

So the Lord Yahweh
    will cause salvation (lit: righteousness) to grow
    and praise before all the nations.

The unconditional announcement of salvation continues. There
are, to be sure, two allusions in this oracle to the separation Yahweh will make between the faithful and unfaithful: in v 2, Yahweh comes in his day of vengeance, which reminds one of 59:17
(cf. 34:8); and in v 8, he describes himself as a lover of justice
and as a hater of sacrifices offered by those who rob others, which
reminds us of ch. 58. Yet the distinction between the faithful and
unfaithful, so common to chs. 56-59, is not pursued in this oracle,
and deliverance and a transformation of fortunes are held out to
Judah as a whole. Indeed, the oracle envisions a universal salvation, in which all nations will share.

Who speaks in this oracle? It has been common to describe vv
1-3 as an individual's account of his prophetic call, and Trito-
Isaiah is then identified as an individual prophet. But the speaker
is not an individual here, but the faithful Levitical-prophetic
community, which here takes on the role of Second Isaiah's Servant. They are, as in Isa. 49:6, that portion in Israel sent "to restore the preserved of Israel" and to be "a light to the nations."
As in 57:1-2, Third Isaiah is deliberately attributing to the Levitical-prophetic community the functions of Second Isaiah's Servant. The connections made are numerous. Both the Servant and
the Levitical-prophetic community are anointed by the Spirit of
Yahweh which gives them power to carry out their task (42:1;
61:1). Both proclaim freedom for the captives (42:7; 61:1; cf.
49:9). The message of both is to announce the favor of Yahweh
(cf. 49:8; 61:2) to those who mourn (cf. 49:13; 61:2) and who are
of a faint spirit (42:3; 61:3). Both messages proclaim that the
desolate heritages will be rebuilt (cf. 49:8; 61:4). Both use the
images of grazing sheep (cf. 49:9; 61:5) and of a marriage (cf.
49:18; 61:11). Both proclamations include the response of joy
and praise (cf. 49:13; 62:10). Trito-Isaiah has taken up Deutero-

Isaiah's pictures of the faithful Servant and applied them to the faithful in its own situation.

Thus, in the first two strophes, vv 1-3 and 4-6, the Levitical-prophetic community speaks, as an individual, in the role of Servant to Judah. In the third strophe, vv 7-9, where we have a change to third person address, Yahweh himself is the speaker, describing the coming transformation of his people's life. In the final strophe, vv 10-11, the whole Judean community responds in praise, also speaking corporately as an individual.

< 1-3 > The Levitical-prophetic Servant community claims no power in and of itself. In its situation in post-exilic Judah, it has no worldly power, any more than the Christian church ever has any worldly power. Its power comes solely from the all-powerful Spirit of Yahweh, which rests upon it (cf. 59:21; Mic. 3:8; Num. 24:2; 2 Sam. 23:2; Zech. 7:12). That Spirit works to send the community to do a seven-fold task (cf. the seven-fold endowment of the Spirit in Isa. 11:2). There are seven infinitives in vv 1c-3, and all depend on the verb "sent."

The Servant community is sent to announce good tidings to the poor (cf. 11:4; 29:19), that is, good news to the struggling community of Judah. The word for "good tidings" is taken from Second Isaiah (40:9; 41:27; 52:7; cf. Nah. 1:15) and is the term from which we get our word "gospel" or "good news." What those good tidings are is then spelled out in the infinitive clauses that follow:

healing for those who are brokenhearted for whatever reason or over whatever loss (cf. 42:3);

freedom for those who are captive, not only literally captive in exile still (cf. 45:13) but figuratively captive to any circumstance (cf 49:9, 25);

comfort (cf. 49:13; 40:1) for those who mourn (cf. 57:18; 60:1, 20);

the receipt of fine *clothing* ("turban") and festival *unguent* ("oil of joy") in exchange for the dust poured on the head and the veils worn over the face in ceremonies of lamentation for the dead (cf. Jer. 31:13);

praise on their lips for blessings received, instead of listlessness and despair over their situation; and

the gift of a *new name* by which they shall be called: firm and mighty "oaks of salvation," planted by Yahweh himself in order to bring glory to himself in the eyes of all nations (cf. 44:23; Jer. 17:8; Pss. 1:3; 52:8).

Most important in the list of infinitive phrases is that one in v 2ab, however: the Servant community is sent to proclaim the year of Yahweh's favor (cf. 49:8; 60:10). In short, a new era is dawning, in which Yahweh's judgment on his people will be turned aside; he will repay Judah's enemies, and bestow on his sinful and undeserving people nothing but good.

< 4-6 > expand still further on these glowing promises. Not only will Jerusalem be rebuilt (cf. 44:26; 45:13; 49:17; 60:10), but all the devastation Israel has known through the years of warfare and conquest will be replaced by new cities with new inhabitants (cf. 58:12; 49:8; 60:15; Ezek. 36:33; Am. 9:14). As in 60:10 and 60:14 (cf. 14:2), those who formerly oppressed Israel and held it captive will become its servants, while Israel will serve as Yahweh's kingdom of priests (cf. Exod. 19:6; 1 Peter 2:5; Rev. 1:6; 5:10; 20:6), mediating the knowledge of him to the world. The result is that the nations will confess Yahweh as their God also ("our God," v 6c; cf. 56:6). The oracle envisions nothing less than worldwide allegiance to the Lord (cf. 45:14, 22-25). But Israel as Yahweh's priests will have no need to worry about material necessities, for the wealth and abundance of all the nations will sustain its life (cf. 60:5, 11).

< 7-9 > Yahweh himself then takes up the glad announcement. The depth of shame and reproach which Israel knew from the nations round about her is emphasized by saying it was "twofold" (cf. 40:2; 54:4; Jer. 19:8; 25:9, 18; 29:18; Mic. 6:16). There-

fore, when her life is transformed, she will enjoy two-fold abundance in the land (cf. Zech. 9:12) and joyfulness which will never cease (cf. 60:15). Indeed, in fulfillment of the promise to Abraham (Gen. 12:2-3), her descendants will be a blessing in the midst of the earth by which all peoples will bless themselves (cf. 44:3). All peoples will acknowledge that Israel has been favored and saved by Yahweh (cf. 45:22-25; 41:20; 49:6-7; 52:13-14; 53:10; 60:3, 14).

< 10-11 > In the final strophe, the Judean community is therefore shown breaking forth in joyful response to these happy announcements, exulting that it has been clothed with Yahweh's salvation like a bride or groom clothed with their wedding garments (cf. 49:18). The metaphor of Israel as the bride of God was used previously by Hosea and Jeremiah, and that figure will reappear in ch. 62; but here the figure of the bridegroom is also employed of Israel. The way Trito-Isaiah uses this metaphor shows its authors' great creativity. In Isa. 49:18, from which Trito-Isaiah takes the figure, the "garment" with which redeemed Israel is clothed is her children returning from exile. Here this "clothing" is generalized to refer to Yahweh's entire act of salvation. And in ch. 62, the authors will use the figure in still a different way (see below). The variation on the marriage metaphor exhibits a lively use of past tradition and the most urgent employment of metaphorical speech to picture the coming salvation.

< 11 > Finally, the Judean community is pictured confessing its faith in Yahweh's fidelity to his promises. Once again the figure of speech is taken from Second Isaiah (55:10-11) and used creatively. The people confess that as surely as the earth brings forth vegetation, so surely will the Lord Yahweh (repeating the title from v 1 to close the unit) cause his salvation (cf. Ps. 85:11) and praise in Israel to spring up before the eyes of all the nations as a witness to them (cf. 60:18; for the figure of a garden, cf. 58:11; Jer. 31:12).

The authors of this oracle are here holding out before Judah the vision of what she can become under God—nothing less than the center of the kingdom of God on earth. But the authors say nothing about how this salvation is to come. It is connected with no historical movement of nations, no actual political or economic changes in Judah's fortunes under the Persian empire. Second Isaiah's soaring hymns of promise had been connected with the historical rise of Cyrus of Persia. Here in Trito-Isaiah, we have a vision of salvation unconnected with Judah's actual circumstances.

For this reason, Paul Hanson has maintained that we have in Third Isaiah the pre-stage of prophetic apocalyptic, in which the vision of the glorious future is loosed from its connection with historical realities. And indeed, one cannot help wondering how these glorious promises were received by the struggling Judean community. Had they not heard them all before, from Second Isaiah? The promises had not come to pass in the actual return from exile. Why should the Judeans put any more credence in the promises of salvation now, especially when such words were being proclaimed by a little band of despised and rejected Levites and prophets? The Judeans must have been as skeptical about this gospel as we are of the message of some ragged figure on a city street, who carries a sign proclaiming the end of the world. When did such promises ever come to pass for Judah?

The only answer we can make is to point to that account of the beginning of the ministry of Jesus of Nazareth, recorded in Luke 4:16-19, which tells of the day he stood up in his hometown synagogue and read the opening lines of this passage from Trito-Isaiah. After Jesus had closed the book and sat down, he said to those in the synagogue, "Today this scripture has been fulfilled in your hearing" (vv 20-21). In similar fashion, Matt. 11:5 (= Luke 7:22) records that Jesus used a portion of this oracle to point to himself as the awaited Messiah. In other words, the gospel writers saw these promises, proclaimed by Trito-Isaiah, to have been fulfilled in the activity of the final Suffering Servant, Jesus Christ.

There is a long stretch of time between the sixth century B.C. postexilic Judean community and the appearance of Jesus of Nazareth, and the fact that the Bible knows of no other fulfillment of Trito-Isaiah's words than that given by God in Christ, shrouds in mystery the way God works in history to keep his Word. His ways are truly not our ways and his thoughts not our thoughts, and we cannot calculate aforetime the manner in which God will work out his purposes. But the fulfillment of this oracle in Jesus Christ also warns us against terming any Word of God preserved in the Old Testament by Israel as merely visionary or unrelated to reality. The people of Israel still hope in this Word today. We in the church believe we have seen its fulfillment, and we are stewards of that mysterious working of God.

It should further be noted that in the Bible, the promises of God always have a proleptic effect. That is, once a promise of God is proclaimed, the power of that very Word enables its recipients to live, at least in a partial manner, as if the Word of promise had already been fulfilled. For example, Israel never saw the kingdom of God come on earth, and yet the Enthronement Psalms (47, 96-99) witness to the fact that Israel knew in its finest worship the joy and security of the universal kingdom already come. Similarly, the Christian Church has not yet experienced the resurrection and the final messianic banquet, and yet there can be no doubt that through the proclamation of their certain coming, in our worship and at the Lord's Supper, we already experience the first fruits of their power and gladness. The power of the very Word of promised resurrection enables us to lead new lives. The promise works its fulfillment in our present situation even before it is finally fulfilled.

So it was, too, with this word of Trito-Isaiah. It was preserved by Israel after Trito-Isaiah's time not only because Israel saw it as a promise for the future, but also because it worked its liberating and saving effects in sixth century B.C. Judah and in every succeeding generation. Those who heard these words were in fact freed and comforted and made joyful in their generation. God's future became their present. And the fact that these words have been fully realized in the person of Jesus Christ only confirms Israel's experience for our faith.

This oracle of Trito-Isaiah's is therefore, indeed, good news. It proclaims to all who are bound by any circumstance that there is freedom to be had in God;

- to all who mourn and are brokenhearted that they may greatly rejoice in the Lord;
- to all who are faint of spirit that there is quickening renewal for their lives;
- to all who are poor that God will reward abundantly;
- to all who are homeless, helpless, rootless that their lives may be firmly planted;
- to all who are without God in the world that he favors them and comes to them in mercy.

Above all, for us his church, God makes us his people in Jesus Christ, his kingdom of priests, his witnesses to the world of this good news. Surely our only response can be those closing lines of this oracle, "I will greatly rejoice in Yahweh . . . for he has clothed me in garments of salvation!"

Isaiah 62:1-9

1 For the sake of Zion I will not keep silent,
    and for the sake of Jerusalem I will not remain still,
    until her deliverance (lit: righteousness) goes forth like
        morning brightness,
    and her salvation flames likes a torch.
2 And the nations shall see your deliverance,
    and all kings your glory.
  And you shall be called by a new name
    which the mouth of Yahweh will appoint you.

3   And you shall become a beautiful crown in the hand
        of Yahweh,
    and a royal diadem in the palm of your God.

    ————

4   You will no longer be called "Forsaken,"
    and your land will no longer be called,
        "Desolate Waste;"
    But you will be called, "My Delight is in Her",
    and your land, "Married."
    For Yahweh delights in you,
        and your land will be married.
5   For as a young man marries a virgin,
        your sons shall marry you;
    and as a bridegroom rejoices over a bride,
        your God will rejoice over you.

    ————

6   Upon your walls, O Jerusalem,
        I will set watchmen.
    All the day and all the night,
        they shall never be silent.
    You who remember Yahweh:
        never rest,
7   and give him no rest
        until he establishes
    and makes Jerusalem
        a praise in the earth!

    ————

8   Yahweh has sworn by his right hand
        and by his mighty arm:
    "I will not again give your grain
        as food for your enemies;
    and foreigners shall not drink your wine
        for which you labored.
9   For those who harvest it shall eat [it],
        and they shall praise Yahweh;
    and those who gather it shall drink [it]
        in my holy courts.

The structure of this salvation oracle is quite regular, consisting
of four strophes of five full lines each, and beginning and ending
with reference to Zion. Some commentators join vv 10-12 to this
oracle, because v 12, like v 4, promises that Zion will no longer be
forsaken and will be given a new name. But the new name has
already been given in v 4, and v 12 gives a different name. It is
better to see vv 10-12 as the oracle intended to sum up and close
the entire middle section, chs. 60-62, of the prophetic book, just
as 59:21 closed the first section.

< 1-3 > One of the principal functions of a prophet, according
to the Old Testament, was that of intercession for the people
before God (cf. Deut. 9:13-29; Amos 7:1-6; Jer. 7:16; 14:11; 15:1;
Ezek. 13:5; 22:30), and here in v 1 the prophetic community reas-
sures Judah that it will never cease praying for her life before God
until her salvation comes. This is paralleled in v 6 by the figure
of the prophets at watchmen, again a familiar figure for the
prophet in the Old Testament (cf. Jer. 6:17; Ezek. 3:17; 33:7; Isa.
52:8; Hab. 2:1). The prophets will station themselves on Jerusalem's walls, when the walls are rebuilt, and will watch for Yahweh's return to Zion: Trito-Isaiah is drawing on the Isaianic tradition of 52:7-9, though as always, the tradition is somewhat
altered. Indeed, the prophetic community will give Yahweh no
rest. They will hammer on his door in prayer, as it were (cf. Luke
11:5-13); they will continually pester Yahweh (cf. Luke 18:1-8).
The Lord has been silent (cf. Isa. 42:14; 57:11), and so the prophetic intercessors will never be silent, until Yahweh breaks his
silence and saves his people by returning to them.

This reassurance was perhaps intended to answer the skepticism
of the Judean community about the grand promises of salvation
offered in the two preceding oracles. As we noted in connection
with 61:1-11, there was no reason whatsoever for the beleaguered
inhabitants of Jerusalem to believe the promise held out to them
by the Levitical-prophetic community, and here those "who
remember Yahweh" (v 6e) reassure the Judeans that they will

pray and pray without ceasing until Yahweh remembers Zion.
That the Levitical-prophetic community offers such continual
intercession, despite the calumny heaped upon it by the Judeans,
is testimony to their pure love for their people and for God. Only
those who are pure in heart can exercise such selfless forgiveness
for the wrong done to them and seek the good of those who have
persecuted them (cf. Matt. 5:11-12). We see here a model of how
the Christian community is to love its enemies (Matt. 5:43-48).

The salvation for which the prophets pray is pictured in terms
similar to those of 60:1-3. Once again a figure of light is used (v 1;
cf. 50:10; 58:8, 10; 59:9; 60:19-20), though "morning brightness"
and "torch" are two new words in Trito-Isaiah's rich vocabulary.
And once again, the nations are drawn to Judah's light ("glory,"
v 2b, which has the meaning of reflected effulgence here, as
in 60:3).

Further, a new name will be given Judah (v 2cd), and this has
been a frequent motif in Trito-Isaiah (cf. 58:12; 60:14, 18; 61:3,
6, 9). But the difference is that this is now a new name that Yahweh will give her. Previously the new name has been affixed by
the nations or by Judah herself; now it is to be given by God; and
that means that it will have everlasting significance. A name,
according to the Old Testament, is the bearer of essence, and
when a name is changed, a new essence and existence are given
(cf. Gen. 17.5; 15-16; 32.28; 1 Sam. 25:25, etc.). Yahweh will
appoint a new name for Judah, signifying a fundamental change
in Judah's nature and circumstances.

The new name is not given immediately. Instead, in v 3, its
content is hinted at by the comparison of Zion to a beautiful
crown, held in the hand of her king, or to a jewel, resting in God's
sovereign hand (cf. 49:16; 59:1; 60:21). The figure draws on
ancient oriental iconography, in which the tutelary deity of a city
was represented as a king, crowned by the city walls of his realm.
But the Isaianic tradition shrinks from the pagan representation
(cf. 28:5), and here in v 3, Yahweh holds Jerusalem in his hand—
a figure expressive of the most tender care of the king for his city.

< 4-6 >   Now the new name for Judah is given. No longer will
Yahweh call her "Forsaken" (cf. 49:14; 54:6; 60:15) and "Desolate Waste" (cf. 49:19; 52:9; 60:18), thereby leveling his judgments against her. Now Yahweh will call her "Hepzibah" ("My
delight is in her") and "Beulah" ("Married"; this is the passage
from which our expression "Beulah land" is taken). These new
names will express the new reality: Yahweh will delight in Judah,
i.e., he will now show favor toward her rather than wrath (cf.
60:10; 61:2).

Many commentators emend v 5b to read, "Your Builder shall
marry you," and they see Yahweh as the bridegroom of the land,
married to it. This would make v 5ab parallel, then, with v 5cd.
But the marriage of the god to his country was a distinctly
Canaanite mythological usage; the god was the "ba'al," husband
and owner, of the land (cf. Hos. 2:16-17), who impregnated it
with fertility. The Old Testament usually avoids such pagan con-
cepts, and it does so here in v 5. Not God, but Judah's returning
sons will "marry," that is, farm the land once again. All can enter
into that possession of the land promised to the faithful (57:13),
if they will trust Yahweh's promises (cf. 60:21; 61:7). Then the
marriage metaphor of 61:10 is altered to picture Yahweh as the
bridegroom of his restored people, who rejoices over his bride
(cf. 54:1, 4-8; Jer. 32:41; Zeph. 3:17). Once again the figure is
expressive of the most tender desire of Yahweh: he is like a young
man with a new wife—solicitous, adoring, enraptured. Such
anthropomorphisms of the Old Testament afford us pictures of
God that are breathtaking in the love they portray.

That it is Yahweh who will give Judah her new name is an
important motif in the Old Testament. In the picture of universal
sin, exhibited in the nations' pride at the Tower of Babel (Gen.
11:1-9), humankind wishes "to make a name" for itself (v 4), to
guarantee its own security and immortality (the essence of the
person was passed down from father to son in the name, according to Hebrew anthropology). The picture is not too different
from our preoccupation with our own success and fame and

image. And Yahweh judges such pride of human beings, according to the Babel story, scattering them abroad on the earth and confusing their language, so that all human community becomes impossible. However, he then sets out in the call of Abraham, in Gen. 12:1-3, to make a new people, whose name *he* will make great (Gen. 12:2)—true human significance is given only by God. Here in Isa. 62:2, then, the promise to Abraham and his descendants is renewed. Yahweh will give Judah a name, so that Jerusalem will become a source of praise in the earth, v 7 (cf. 61:9; Deut. 28:10).

< 8-9 > These promises of salvation are made sure by Yahweh's solemn oath, quoted here. There is no more certain guarantee that can be given than for Yahweh to swear by his own everlasting, unchangeable nature (cf. 45:23; 54:9), and here in v 8, he swears in accordance with his saving right hand (cf. 59:1; 60:21) and his mighty, rescuing arm (cf. 40:10-11; 48:14; 51:5, 9). Never again will the enemies of Judah overrun her land, and eat and drink her produce. To understand the full force of that promise, we must realize that the covenant ceremony in Israel included a recital of blessings and curses—promised blessings for those keeping the covenant, certain curses for those breaking it (cf. Deut. 28; Lev. 26). One such curse was this: the consumption by enemies of the fruits of Israel's labor (cf. Deut. 28:30-33; Lev. 26:16). Thus that which is promised here in vv 8-9 is the full restoration of the covenant with Yahweh; and the meal pictured in v 9 is the communion meal of the covenant, to be celebrated in the presence of Yahweh in the rebuilt temple on Zion. This is a picture of Yahweh returned and dwelling in the midst of his people.

It should be pointed out in connection with this communion meal and Israel's enjoyment of the fruits of her own labor, that one of the benefits of the renewal of our covenant with God in the Christian church, through the death and resurrection of Jesus Christ—celebrated every time we partake of the Lord's Supper (cf. 1 Cor. 11:23-25)—is precisely the assurance that our labor will not be in vain (1 Cor. 15:58). No longer will our lives be marked by futility and our work overcome by evil. In the new covenant through Jesus Christ, our labor will bear its fruit. Surely such an assurance is good news in the midst of our transitory world, where every good accomplishment seems to fall victim to evil's influence, and every pure and lovely attainment seems swept away by ugliness and corruption. God's covenant in Jesus Christ will stand, and every good life will not be in vain. That is a promise that gives renewed hope and motivation for Christian living.

Isaiah 62:10-12

10   Go through! Go through the gates!
       Clear a way for the people!
       Prepare! Prepare the highway!
       Free it from stones!
       Lift up a flag over the peoples!

―――――

11   Behold! Yahweh has proclaimed
       to the end of the earth:
       "Say to the daughter of Zion, 'Behold!
       Your salvation comes'!"
       Behold! his recompense with him
       and his reward before him!

―――――

12   And they shall be called, "The Holy People,"
       "Redeemed of Yahweh."
       And you shall be called, "Sought Out,"
       "City-Not-Forsaken."

This salvation oracle forms the end-piece for the entire second section, chs. 60-62, just as 59:21 was the closing promise for chs. 56-59. It is made up almost entirely of quotations or paraphrases of Second Isaiah. Verse 10 is similar to 40:3; 10e recalls 49:22 (cf.

11:10, 12); v 11 is similar to 40:9-11, 11a-d is like 48:20, and 11ef
quotes 40:10cd word for word; v 12d recalls 41:17; 42:16 and 54:6.
However, though the words are similar, the meanings are quite
different from those found in Second Isaiah.

Three questions are prompted by this oracle. To whom is it
addressed? For whom is the way being prepared? Who are "they"
in v 12? The answers to these questions determine the meaning
of the oracle, and scholars have differed in their answers. The
following seem best to me.

< 10 > The summons to prepare a way is very much like the
summons in 57:14, but here it is issued to the inhabitants of Jerusalem and Judah as a whole. As Yahweh's saved people, the
Judeans are now to fling wide their gates (which is also the
thought of 60:11) and to prepare a smooth road for foreign peoples (described by both singular "the people" 10b, and plural "the
peoples" 10e), in order that all nations may stream toward Jerusalem. Indeed, a flag or signal is to be lifted up in order to guide
the foreign peoples toward Jerusalem (cf. 49:22).

< 11 > The nature of the signal is then described: it is Yah-
weh's proclamation of Israel's salvation to the end of the earth
(cf. 49:6). Her salvation, in the form of Yahweh's return to her
(LXX and Vulgate both read "Savior" for "salvation"), comes
(cf. 56:1; 51:5; Zech. 9:9), and that is the signal to the foreign
peoples that Yahweh alone is God and that therefore they too
should worship him alone. Thus they will stream toward Zion
to do homage to Yahweh, and that is the "reward" and "recompense" referred to in 11e and 11f. The reward of Yahweh's act of
salvation is the universal acknowledgment of his lordship.

In short, this oracle forms the companion piece to the opening
section, 60:1-22, where we find exactly the same thought of Yahweh's salvation of Zion and the streaming of all peoples toward
her reflected light. As did Deutero-Isaiah before him, Trito-Isaiah
often begins and ends a section with the same motif.

< *12* > The question still remains, however, who are "they" in
v 12a, and I differ radically with most scholars here. I believe the
people who are to be called "the Holy People" (cf. Exod. 19:6;
Deut. 7:6; Isa. 4:3; 1 Peter 2:9) and the "Redeemed of Yahweh"
are the foreigners who come to Jerusalem. As in the oracle in
56:1-8, Trito-Isaiah here breaks all nationalistic and exclusivistic
bounds and sees the vision of a united humanity, worshiping in
"a house of prayer for all peoples," before the sovereign Lord of
all the earth. It is, in short, a vision of the coming kingdom of
God on earth (cf. similar universalistic views in Isa. 2:2-4; 11:9,
10; 44:5; 45:22-25). And the means by which it is to be achieved
—namely through the salvation and exaltation of Israel—is precisely that which is found in Isa. 52:13—53:12 (cf. 61:9; 62:2).
Trito-Isaiah holds out to the whole of Judah and Jerusalem the
possibility still of joining the Levitical-prophetic community in
the role of performing the functions of the Servant of the Lord
in bringing salvation to the world.

Because all nations will come to Jerusalem, she shall therefore
be called, v 12c and 12d, "Sought Out" and "City-Not-Forsaken"
(cf. 60:14-15; Jer. 30:17). The section closes, as it began in ch. 60,
with the picture of abundant life in the kingdom. It is that picture
—that glorious vision of the future redeemed by God—which
Trito-Isaiah's authors want their people to live by and trust.

One is reminded of the saying of the One who was forsaken,
and yet who finally fulfilled the mission of the Suffering Servant:
". . . I, when I am lifted up from the earth, will draw all men to
myself" (John 12:32). By the exaltation of his Suffering Servant,
God works his redemption of the world.

Unfolding the Message

PART III Isaiah 63-66

Isaiah 63:1-6

1 Who is this coming from Edom,
    [in] deep red garments, from Bozrah—
    this [figure], glorious (majestic) in his apparel,
      marching in the greatness of his strength?
    [It is] I, acting in deliverance (lit: righteousness),
      [I], great to save!

———

2 Why is your apparel red,
    and your garments like a treader's in the wine-press?
3 A wine-press I have trod alone,
    and there was no one with me from the peoples;
and I trod them in my anger,
    and I trampled them in my wrath;
and their life-blood (lit: juice) squirted on my garments,
    and I stained all my apparel;
4 for the day of vengeance was in my heart,
    and the year of my redemption has come.

———

5   When I looked, there was no helper,
        and I was astonished! There was no one to count
            (lean) on!
    So my [own] arm brought me victory (lit: saved me),
        and my wrath sustained (upheld) me;
6   and I crushed peoples in my anger,
        and I made them drunk in my wrath;
    and I poured out their life-blood (lit: juice) on the ground.

In chapters 60-62, the Levitical-prophetic community offered to all in Judah and Jerusalem, and indeed to all the world, the promise of Yahweh's salvation. But every great preacher knows that to move a people, the people must be able to see what is being proclaimed. Here in this magnificent poem, which has so greatly influenced the literature and songs of the Western world, the Trito-Isaianic community enables its countrymen to see—to see Yahweh the victorious Warrior coming—marching—speaking (v 1); to see Yahweh the lonely Conqueror trodding out "the grapes of wrath"; to see God in sovereign might, victorious over all his enemies.

The poem is intimately connected with all that has gone before. The promised destruction of Israel's enemies in 60:12 is here pictured as event of the past. The year of redemption and day of vengeance announced in 61:2 (cf. 34:8; 35:4; 49:8; Jer. 51:6) have now arrived. The prophetic watchers on the walls of Jerusalem, who in 62:6-7 searched the horizon for Yahweh's coming to his people to redeem them, now behold him near enough to shout out questions to him (for the form, cf. 21:11-12). The Divine Warrior of 59:16-20 is here given figure and shape. The prophetic community now verbally draws before Judah's eyes the picture of its returning Savior, and what an overwhelming, totally strange picture it is both to them and to us!

< 1 >   A solitary, majestic, apparently enormous Warrior, sways (such is the force of *tz'h* in 1d) back and forth as he strides out

of the south toward Jerusalem. He is without weapons or accompanying army. He is clothed in a robe and leather armor; his garments spattered with a purple-red not their own. The watchers on the walls of Jerusalem call out to him to identify himself. But no name is necessary when he reveals his mission: he comes to deliver, mighty to save. The figure can only be God himself.

< 2-4 > The watchers on the walls persist in their questioning. Why are God's garments like those who tread the juice out of the grapes in the wine-trough at harvest time (cf. Joel 3:13; Lam. 1:15)? And the dreadful answer comes back from God: because he has trodden his enemies in his wrath (cf. 22:5; 28:3; Mic. 7:10), as in a winepress (the word is used elsewhere only in Hag. 2:16), and their lifeblood (literally, juice, to preserve the figure of grapes) has spattered on his robe and sandals. God's enemies have now been destroyed in his day of reckoning, a day planned from the first in his purpose (= "heart" v 4a). All opposition to him is gone.

< 5-6 > The final strophe emphasizes, however, that God won his victory alone. He had no helper, no other soldiers, no confederates from foreign nations (cf. "peoples," v 3b) or from Judah to rely on. His own arm gained the victory in the slaughter, and his wrath against the evil of his opponents kept him going in the fray, even though he was astonished that there were no human beings who would join cause with him. He, and he alone, defeated the forces of evil, so that they reeled like drunken men before his anger (cf. 29:9; 51:17, 21-23; Jer. 25:15-29; Hab. 2:16) and spilled out their juices on the earth and died. And now, having defeated all enemies, Yahweh comes to Judah to save (cf. Zeph. 3:17). But her deliverance will mean, as in the preceding chapters, the salvation also of the rest of the world.

What are we to make of such a bloody, slaughtering, conquering God? The figure of the trodden grapes, with their juice spattering out, which is used to portray God crushing out the life of his enemies, is appalling in our eyes, going far beyond the portrayal of the Divine Warrior in 59:16-20 (see that section for a fuller discussion). This poetry bears a power which 59:16ff. lacked, and it shows the rhetorical force of which the Trito-Isaianic community was capable. Here the message is driven home in all its awfulness: God who comes to save is terrible against those who oppose him.

Edom refers in the passage not to that specific nation, although it is elsewhere in the Old Testament judged for its treachery toward Judah after the fall of Jerusalem in 587 B.C. (cf. Jer. 49:7-22; Ezek. 25:12-14; 35:1-12; Amos 1:11-12; Ob. 1:21; Mal. 1:2-5; Ps. 137:7). Rather, Edom stands for the evil of all the foreign nations, as in Isa. 34:5, 8-9, and the name is deliberately chosen for a word play: "Edom" is similar to 'adom, the Hebrew word for "red," just as the capital of Edom, Bozrah, may suggest bozer, "vintager."

Certainly we should be warned by this passage if we hinder or oppose God's purposes, for the Trito-Isaianic community intended the oracle to warn all enemies of God. But principally that community intended this victory song to be a source of comfort for the people of God. God will destroy all evil opposition to his cause in the world. His enemies' strength is as nothing before his might. He can crush opponents as easily as a man can crush the grapes in the winepress with his bare feet. In a world such as ours, full of violence and injustice and cold indifference to the ways of God, that is a source of comfort. God will win the battle and come to save his people. "I will not leave you desolate," his Son promised us; "I will come to you" (John 14:18). And then he went out and did battle on Golgotha and in the tomb with the forces of darkness, and manifested his triumph over them on the third day at dawn. Surely the familiar *Battle Hymn of the Republic,* based on this poem, catches the mood of that triumph.

We should remember, further, that the emphasis of the poem is on God's lonely victory. Whereas the Zadokite priestly party implements its policies with the approval and support of Persia,

Yahweh uses no empire to accomplish his triumph over wrong. You will not be saved by Persia, Trito-Isaiah is saying to Judah, but by God alone, and it is to his power and his will that you must look for deliverance. Contrary to its assessment by some commentators, the poem has not abandoned the historical context in which it is spoken; it simply rejects the view of the Zadokites and their followers who believe that human governments and human programs can bring in the kingdom of God. The Trito-Isaianic community did not believe that the ideal programs constructed in exile by the Zadokites and priestly writers and Ezekiel's disciples could guarantee either Yahweh's favor or the security of the future. That future, they maintained, depended solely on the mercy and might of a sovereign God. It is that might, over against all rebellion against him, and that mercy, determined to save his own, which are set forth in this victory song in unforgettable fashion.

Isaiah 63:7—64:12

7 The covenant deeds of Yahweh I will call to remembrance,
      the praiseworthy acts of Yahweh,
   all [the good things] Yahweh has awarded us,
      and [his] great good to the house of Israel,
   which he has awarded us according to his mercies
      and according to the abundance of his covenant love.
8 For he said, "Surely, they are my people,
      sons who will not deal falsely."
   And he became to them a Savior.
9   In all their affliction
   he was afflicted, and the angel
      of his Presence saved them.
   In his love and in his compassion,
      he redeemed them;
   and he took them up and he carried them
      all the days of old.
10 Yet they disobeyed and they grieved

his holy spirit;
so he turned and became to them an enemy;
he himself made war against them.

11   But I will call to remembrance the days of old—
[of] Moses [and of] my people.
Where is he who brought up from the sea
the shepherds of his flock?
Where is the one who put in their midst
his holy spirit,
12   who caused to go at Moses' right hand
his glorious arm;
who divided the waters before them
to make for himself an everlasting name;
13   who caused them to pass through the great deep?
Like a horse in the desert,
they did not stumble.
14   Like cattle
going down into the valley,
the spirit of Yahweh brought them rest.
Thus you led your people,
to make for yourself a glorious name.

15   Look down from heaven and see,
from your holy and glorious habitation!
Where are your zeal and your might,
the yearning of your inmost parts?
For your mercies toward [us] (lit: me) restrain themselves.
16   For you are our Father,
but Abraham knows us not,
and Israel recognizes us not.
You, Yahweh! [You are] our Father!
Our Redeemer from of old is your name!
17   Why do you cause us to wander,
Yahweh, from your ways?
[Why do you] harden our hearts so that we do not
fear you?

Return for the sake of your servants,
the tribes of your inheritance!
18   For a little while your holy people possessed [it];
[now] our oppressors trample your sanctuary.
19   We have become like those of old
over whom you did not rule,
like those not called by your name.

64:1   O that you would rend the heavens—come down—
before you the mountains would quake,
2   like a fire kindling brushwood,
and like a flame boiling waters—
to make known your name to your adversaries!
Before you the nations would tremble!
3   When you do terrible deeds we do not expect,
[when] you come down, the mountains quake before you.
4   In olden times they had never heard
[and] we have never heard,
nor has eye ever seen
a god besides you,
who acts for those who await him,
5   who joyfully meets anyone who conforms to your order
(lit: does right)
and all those who remember your ways.

Behold! you were angry, and we sinned
a long time. Shall we be saved?
6   For we have become like one unclean—all of us!—
and our good deeds (lit: righteousness) stained like a
menstrual rag.
And we wither like a leaf—all of us!—
and our iniquities, like a wind, bear us away.
7   And there is no one who calls on your name,
and who rouses himself to hold fast to you;
for you have hidden your face from us,
and you have let us melt away (faint) in the grip
(lit: hand) of our iniquities.

---

8 But you! Yahweh!
    Our Father you are!
   We are the clay,
    and you are our Potter
    and [we are the] works of your hand—all of us!
9 Be not angry, Yahweh, to extremes,
    and do not forever remember iniquity!
   Behold! Look! [We are] your people—all of us!
10   Your holy cities have become a desert.
   Zion has become a desert,
    Jerusalem a desolation.
11   Our holy and glorious house
    where our fathers praised you
   has been burned by fire,
    and all our precious things have become a desolation.
12   Given all these things, will you restrain yourself, Yahweh?
    Will you keep silent and afflict us to extremes?

On the face of it, this is a communal lament, much like Ps. 44 or 74 or 79, uttered by a prophet on behalf of the worshiping community, which has gathered together in a day of prayer and fasting to implore Yahweh's help. As such, it has something of the communal lament's structure:

   a) a recounting of Yahweh's saving deeds in the past, 63:7-14 (cf. Ps. 44:1-8);

   b) the detailing of the community's present desperate situation, 63:15-19 (cf. Ps. 44:9-22);

   c) the petition for help, 64:1-12 (cf. Ps. 44:23-26).

It may well be that the Levitical-prophetic community has borrowed phrases from actual communal laments uttered by the postexilic community. Certainly this passage is intended to be an example of the intercessions offered by the prophetic watchmen mentioned in 62:6.

But this is also a prayer uttered by a group—namely, the Levitical-prophetic community—who are sure that they know why Yahweh has not come to Judah's aid. The reason for Yahweh's

absence, for his hiding his face (63:7c), has been stated very
clearly before in 59:1-20: the sins of the Judean community and
especially of its Zadokite priestly leaders have made a separation
between Judah and her God (cf. 59:2). This prayer is therefore
first of all a complaint against the machinations of the Zadokite
group and a plea for deliverance from the Zadokite "oppressors"
(63:18) and from the effects of their evil ways on the life of Judah
as a whole. It is the polemical prayer of a small group, though it
borrows the form and phrases of the communal lament. It does,
however, go beyond the Zadokites' sin to delve deeper into the
theological reasons for Judah's continuing unfaithfulness, and in
doing so, it avoids the extremes of self-righteousness and fanati-
cism and joins common cause with the people as a whole.

< 63:7-14 > The passage opens with a recital of the saving
deeds of Yahweh, which is longer than most such recitals in the
communal laments and which could almost form a historical
Psalm in itself. Yahweh is spoken of in the third person and not
addressed until 63:14d. The singer recalls (cf. 57:11) the covenant
deeds and love (chesed, v 7a and 7f; cf. 54:8, 10: "everlasting
love," "steadfast love") of Yahweh—that great good (cf. 1 Kings
8:66; Neh. 9:25, 35) with which he has recompensed (cf. 59:18;
62:11) his people through all his years with them. At the heart of
this historical remembrance is the covenant relationship: Yahweh
has said to Israel, "You are my people," which is the first half of
the covenant formulaic proclamation (cf. Exod. 6:7; Jer. 31:33).
That is, through no deserving on her part, Israel has been adopted
by God as his own possession, as his special people, set apart for
his purpose in the world, with her life ordered and guided and
sustained by Yahweh's will for her (Exod. 19:4-6).

This adoption of Israel has taken place in the exodus from
Egypt, and from that time forth, Israel has been Yahweh's
adopted son (changing the gender; cf. Exod. 4:22-23; Deut. 8:5;
Isa. 1:2; Hos. 11:1; Jer. 31:20; Gal. 4:4-7), and Yahweh has been
Israel's Father (cf. Isa. 45:11; Jer. 3:19; 31:9; Mal. 1:6; 2:10;

1 Chron. 29:10). The relation into which Yahweh, in his grace, has entered with his people, is therefore one of the most tender love and care. All of Israel's sufferings have been felt in the divine heart, 63:9. When his son fell into slavery, Yahweh bought him back with the redemption price (cf. Lev. 25:47ff.; Isa. 43:3-4). Yahweh, the divine Father, has picked up and carried his child time after time, 63:9 (cf. Isa. 46:3-4; Hos. 11:3).

The expectation of Yahweh has been, therefore, that Israel would respond in the love and obedience of a faithful son to his fatherly love and care. As with so many of the prophetic books, the history of Yahweh's gracious acts toward his people is rehearsed to show the reasonableness of Yahweh's demands on Israel (cf. Amos 2:9-11; Hos. 11:1-4; Mic. 6:3-5; Jer. 2:1-3, 4-8; Isa. 5:1-4). And this history of mercy is then contrasted with Israel's perfidy, 63:10. Despite all of Yahweh's merciful deeds, Israel has rebelled against its Father, in acts of disloyalty and disobedience which are incomprehensible (cf. Jer. 8:4-7), just as our forgetfulness and rebellion against God are incomprehensible in the light of his love in Jesus Christ.

The effect of Israel's disobedience has been grief within the divine Spirit (63:10; cf. Gen. 6:6), grief which penetrated to the very heart of his holy Godhead (cf. Luke 19:41-44) and which made it necessary for God to assert his authority as Father and Lord. If he truly is the Lord over our lives, he can do no other than put down our rebellion against him (cf. Amos 3:2; Jer. 5:7-9; Ezek. 20:33). The God who is always Father to Israel therefore himself became their enemy, and waged that warfare against them of which we have spoken in relation to 59:15-20 (see above). That warfare resulted in the destruction of Judah and Jerusalem and exile into Babylonia in 587 B.C. God's wrath against his people is not a mere emotion. It results in his active judgment on our lives.

< *63:11-14* > Nevertheless, that is not the end of the divine-human relationship. Judgment is really an act strange and alien

to the nature of God the Father (cf. Isa. 28:21; Hos. 11:8-9), and
the Levitical-prophetic community that prays this lament knows
it is strange and alien. In this second strophe, they therefore re-
hearse once again God's specific acts of mercy, but this time the
rehearsal is used not to show the heinousness of Israel's sin, but
to question Yahweh, though modestly, indirectly, and not in first
person address—one does not properly call into question Yahweh's
actions toward his children (cf. Isa. 45:11). The questioning complaint is simply put in the form of a twofold plaintive "Where?"
(63:11c and e). Where, the community asks, is that God who
performed the deliverance from Egypt, who brought up Moses
and the leaders ("shepherds") of the tribes from slavery, who
divided the waters of the Reed Sea before them with the power
of his Spirit-wind, v 11ef (Exod. 14:21-22; cf. Hag. 2:5) and of
his glorious arm, which was really the power behind Moses' hand
stretched out over the sea (v 12ab; Exod. 14:21)? (In contrast
with v 10, the holy spirit here is not Yahweh's inner nature but
his active, outward power.)

By calling the Reed Sea "the great deep" in v 13a, the community compares the deliverance from Egypt to Yahweh's initial
creation and bounding of the chaotic waters (Gen. 1:2; Isa. 51:9-
10; 11:15), and it says that Yahweh has enabled his people to pass
through on dry land as easily as a horse traverses a flat desert
plain. Then in v 14, the settlement in the land is recalled. Like
cattle going down into the valley to refresh themselves at their
watering-places, Israel has been brought into the promised land
and given rest from its wanderings and enemies (cf. Deut. 3:20;
25:19; 12:9-10; Josh. 21:44; 23:1). Thus Yahweh led his people
(cf. Deut. 32:12)—the singer now dares to address Yahweh directly, v 14de—and these acts of deliverance and leading brought
glory to Yahweh's reputation ("name") in the eyes of all the
world. Throughout the Isaiah corpus, Yahweh is glorified by his
great deeds in Israel (cf. also Matt. 5:16; John 12:28).

< *63:15-19* > In this third strophe, the Levitical-prophetic com-

munity now contrasts Yahweh's past deeds of deliverance with
their own situation as outcasts in Jerusalem. This strophe and the
next (64:1-5b) concentrate very specifically on the scorn and loss
of leadership suffered by the Levitical priests and their followers.
The complaint is that their God of mercy, the God who has always
been a Father to Israel, is no longer acting like their Father and
Redeemer. It is as if he is bottling up all his mercies inside of him,
as if he no longer has any zeal for his lordly cause in the world,
as if he is refusing to exercise his sovereign might on behalf of
his purpose. As in a previous passage (see 57:15), Yahweh is pictured as dwelling in heaven. He therefore is bidden to look down
from his holy and glorious dwelling place (cf. Ps. 68:5), where he
is enthroned above the heaven of heavens (cf. Pss. 113:5-6; 123:1;
Isa. 40:22; 6:1), and to see the condition of his faithful (cf. Deut.
26:15; Ps. 80:14).

The first fact of that condition held up before Yahweh is that
"Abraham knows us not, and Israel recognizes us not" (v 16ab).
This is a direct reference to the banishment of the Levitical priests
and their followers from their positions of leadership and influence in the community. The same fact is referred to in v 18: "for
a little while" the Levites—Yahweh's holy people (cf. Jer. 2:3;
Deut. 7:6; 26:19; 28:9; Exod. 19:6)—possessed the sanctuary, that
is, they served as priests in Israel. But now their "adversaries"
trample the holy site—a metaphor for the Zadokites' idolatrous
and insincere worship (cf. Isa. 1:12). In v 17de, Yahweh is therefore implored to "return" (a term applied to Yahweh as the
Divine Warrior, Num. 10:36; Isa. 52:8) for the sake of his true
followers, his "servants" (once again the Levitical-prophetic community takes on the role of Second Isaiah's servant; see on 57:1-2;
61:1-4), "the tribes of his inheritance," that is, the Levites (cf.
Num. 3:40-45).

That it is the Levitical-prophetic party which is treated here in
the third strophe is made almost incontrovertible by the northern,
Deuteronomic, Jeremianic tradition with which this whole lament
is permeated. Frank Cross, in *Canaanite Myth and Hebrew Epic,*

pp. 195-215, has convincingly shown that the Levitical priesthood claimed its Levitic descent through Moses and was centered in the northern house of Eli at Shiloh, and in the Mushite (Mosaic)-Kenite priesthoods at Dan, Arad, and Kadesh-Naphtali. This Levitic priesthood was therefore intimately connected with the tribal federation and with its invisible Lord of Hosts enthroned above the cherubim of the ark. It was this Levitic priesthood which also found a center at Anathoth, the later home of Jeremiah, when Solomon banished the Mushite Abiathar to Anathoth in favor of the Aaronite, Hebronite priest Zadok (1 Kings 2:26, 35). It was from the preaching of these northern Levitical priests that the Book of Deuteronomy was formed; it was their Mosaic covenant tradition which was consistently supported by the prophets of the north, especially Elijah and Hosea; and it was their Deuteronomic covenant tradition and Josiah's Deuteronomic reform which were championed by the prophet Jeremiah. Thus it is not surprising that we have in this lament of Isa. 63:7—64:12

- a prominent reference to the covenant tradition, centered in the exodus of the northern Rachel tribes out of Egypt;
- a central role played by Moses;
- the northern Hoseanic-Deuteronomic tradition of Israel as Yahweh's son;
- a reference in 63:9 to the northern E tradition of the angel of Yahweh's presence (cf. Exod. 32:34) (Difficulties in the text of 63:9 give some indication of later tampering, and it should not be emended to favor the Zadokite, southern view, as with Hanson's reading: "Not a messenger, nor an angel, but his own Presence saved them.");
- the Deuteronomic concept of the gift of the land as Israel's "rest";
- the Deuteronomic view of Yahweh's dwelling in heaven;
- the Jeremianic concept of Yahweh's enmity and war against Judah, and

• the Deuteronomic concept of Yahweh's "holy people."

This lament fairly reeks with northern, Mushite, Deuteronomic-Levitic-Jeremianic tradition.

There is, however, also Isaianic tradition in this lament, and 63:17a-c first exhibits it (cf. Isa. 6:9-10; Exod. 10:1-2). Members of the Levitical-prophetic party also acknowledge their own sin in this prayer and they attribute their sin and the sin of the Judeans to Yahweh's own work of hardening their hearts, so that they do not obey him. As First Isaiah was told in his call, part of Yahweh's work of judgment on his sinful people was the very proclamation of a Word which hardened the people's hearts, so that they did not repent and their exile and destruction became inevitable in Yahweh's purpose. According to Trito-Isaiah, Yahweh continues to work in such a manner, hardening their hearts, so that the Judean community brings further judgment on itself in postexilic times. It is finally the only reason Trito-Isaiah can see for the continuing distress of the nation as a whole and for the persistent lack of trust among the people—it is part of Yahweh's plan (cf. Isa. 22:11b). Yahweh is a merciful God in Trito-Isaiah's view, and the continuing ruin of Judah is incomprehensible apart from some purpose God may have for it (cf. Rom. 11:25).

< 64:1-5b > Despite the persecution the Levitic-prophetic community is suffering at the hands of the Zadokites, they therefore also join common cause with the Judeans, and the last three strophes of this prayer of lament (64:1-5b; 64:5c-7; 64:8-12) pray for the good of the Judean community as a whole. Indeed, the Levitical-prophetic party acknowledges, in 64:5b-7, its oneness in sin with its fellow Judeans. The repeated phrase, "all of us," in 64:6a and c, 8e, and 9c emphasizes this oneness. The Levites and prophets do not claim perfection for themselves before God; nor do they cut themselves off from their fellow countrymen in some isolating claim to self-righteousness. They feel themselves bound together in the bundle of life with their countrymen; they con-

tinually pray for their fellows, as we have seen; and here they continue that intercessory prayer appropriate to those who see themselves called to be Yahweh's suffering servants.

Their prayer is to that God who has always ruled over his people and who has made them his own (63:19)—once again a reference to the covenant relationship—and the plea of strophe four, 64:1-5b, is that the sovereign Lords of hosts, enthroned above the heaven of heavens, will cleave the firmament in two—(the arc of the firmament was thought to be solid in ancient Near Eastern cosmology)—and come down (cf. Pss. 18:9; 144:5) in a mighty theophany to save his people from their foreign adversaries. The parallelism with "the nations" in 64:2d shows the reference is now to foreign peoples and not, as previously, to the Zadokite party. The coming of Yahweh to earth is frequently conceived in the Old Testament to be accompanied by cosmological disturbances (cf. Mic. 1:3-4; Nah. 1:3-5; Ps. 68:8), and here the principal picture is of the mountains quaking before him, reminiscent of the exodus (cf. Ps. 114; Matt. 27:51) and of the descent of God to Sinai (cf. Exod. 19:18; Judg. 5:5). But the shaking of the cosmos is paralleled by the trembling of the nations before Yahweh's Presence (cf. Hab. 3:6; Jer. 33:9; Pss. 114:7; 99:1).

This is a fearsome Lord who descends to do terrible deeds, that is, deeds of terrifying and awesome power (cf. Deut. 10:21; Pss. 65:5; 66:3, 5; 106:22), to save his covenant people. This is no gentle deity of sweetness and light, no benign great soul of nature, no projection of human ideals upon the universe, but a God utterly Other than this world ever dreamed of (64:4; cf. 1 Cor. 2:9), totally different from the gods of all other nations; the unexpected (64:3), completely unique Ruler of all. And yet this is the God who, for all his awesome power, stoops to act on behalf of anyone who expects and trusts his action (v 4e—this is the meaning of "awaits him"; cf. 26:8-9; 40:31), and who rejoices over anyone who walks according to his ways (v 5).

< 64:5c-7 > To be sure, Judah has been sinful and Yahweh has

been angry for a very long time (cf. 47:6; 54:8-9). This fifth strophe therefore questions in wistful tones if salvation will ever come. The figure of "uncleanness" for sin, though very graphic here, recalls Isa. 6:5 (cf. Job 15:14-16); and the metaphors of withering (cf. Isa. 40:7-8; Pss. 1:3; 90:5-6) and of being carried away as by a wind (cf. 57:13; Jer. 4:11-12; Ps. 1:4) are frequent in the Old Testament. Verse 6 is not a continuation of the confession of sin, however, but the further complaint that no one can call on Yahweh's name, that is, worship him (cf. 58:2, 9), or hold fast to him (cf. 56:2, 4) because he has hidden his Presence or face (cf. Exod. 33:14) from them (cf. 57:17; 59:2; 45:15; 54:8; 1:15; Deut. 31:18), and given them over to melt away (cf. Ezek. 22:20), that is, to faint, to become weak and lifeless, in the bondage of their iniquities.

< *64:7-11* > Beyond all hopelessness and helplessness, however, there is the fact that God has entered into relation with his people in the past, and it is to that past relationship that Trito-Isaiah appeals in this final strophe. God has been Father to Israel from the time of the exodus on (cf. 63:16). God has created his people in the deliverance from Egypt, like a potter creating an earthenware vessel (cf. 29:16; 45:9; Jer. 18:1-5; 2 Cor. 4:7). God's people are the work of his hand (cf. 60:21; 62:3; Ps. 100:3), delivered, formed, preserved through all the years simply out of his mercy. Will he then turn and destroy that which he has so lovingly made and preserved (cf. Job 10:8)? It would go beyond all his purpose for Israel, to remember her iniquity forever (v 8b; cf. 43:25; Mic. 7:18; Ps. 103:9). It would even be extreme on God's part to go beyond the judgment already leveled against Judah (vv 8a, 11b). Her cities have been destroyed; Jerusalem is a desolation (cf. Isa. 1:7; 6:11); the temple, that holy and glorious house (cf. 60:7; Ps. 79:1) where earlier generations praised the Lord, has been destroyed by fire (cf. 2 Kings 25:9), and so can be a house of praise no longer. Every precious object in the temple has been removed or burned or desecrated (cf. Lam. 1:7, 10-11). Will Yah-

weh therefore go beyond such judgment to judge them even
more? Will he restrain that mercy which is his very nature? Will
he keep silent and not answer their pleas for rescue and not come
to their aid?

Such is the prayer which the stricken members of the covenant
people of God can utter—an appeal to that mercy of God that
made them his people in the first place. Let us draw the analogy
for Christians: God adopted us in Jesus Christ (cf. Gal. 4:4-7);
he became our Father. And nothing can wipe out that act which
has taken place—not our sinfulness, not our lack of faith, not our
captivity to other powers. There is a God of love and mercy who
created us and who redeemed us. And no matter what our situation, he can be appealed to, to act once again to save us as he
saved us when he made us his children. The facts of the past—
God's acts in Jesus Christ—can be recalled and appealed to for
help in the desperate present.

Isaiah 65:1-7

1 I was ready to be sought by those who did not ask
    [for me].
  I was ready to be found by those who did not seek me.
  I said, "Here am I, here am I,"
    to a people who did not call on my name.
2 I spread forth my hands all the day
    to a backsliding people,
  who walk the way [which is] not good,
    after their own devices;
3 [to] the people who provoke me
    before my face continually,
  sacrificing in the gardens
    and burning incense upon the bricks;
4 [to] those who sit in tombs
    and pass the night in secret places;
  [to] those who eat the flesh of swine,
    and [have] a broth [made from] abominable things
      [in] their bowls;

5   [to] those who say, "Stand back!
      Do not come near me, for I am set apart from you!"
    These [people are] smoke in my nostrils,
      a fire burning all the day.

6   Behold! it is written before me:
      I will not keep silent, but I will requite
        ((and I will requite into their bosom))
7   their iniquities and the iniquities of their fathers
      together, says Yahweh.
    Those who burn incense upon the mountains
      and defy me on the heights:
    I will measure out their work upon their head
      and [requite it] into their bosom.

Yahweh now replies to the lament of 63:7—64:12. It was cus-
tomary in the cult of Israel for a priest or cultic prophet to respond
to the lament of a worshiper with an oracle of salvation which
assured the worshiper that his prayer had been heard and that
Yahweh would come speedily to his aid. For this reason, many
of the individual laments end on a note of certainty and trust
(cf. e.g., Ps. 6:8-10). We have here such a prophetic response,
giving the Word of Yahweh. But this reply is not the expected
oracle of salvation; that does not follow until 65:8-25. Instead, this
is an oracle of judgment on the idolatrous Zadokite party and
their followers, much like we found in 57:1-13, and it spells failure
for the Levitical-prophetic efforts to intercede for the Judean
community as a whole. That party had prayed for all the Judeans
and had held out the promise of salvation to the entire postexilic
community, if they would turn from their sinful idolatry and
unjust practices and place their trust in Yahweh's salvation alone.
But the Levitical-prophetic preaching and prayers have not borne
fruit. The Zadokite party remains as stubborn and sinful and
proud as ever. Their eventual doom, therefore, is certain at the
hands of a recompensing God. This oracle spells out the reasons
for that certain fate.

< *1* > In an act of mercy totally unmerited by its recipients, Yahweh made himself available to the Judeans, drawing near to them so that his Presence with them and his guidance for their lives could be known in worship. (To "seek" for Yahweh and to "ask" for him are technical terms denoting inquiry after an oracle of Yahweh from a priest or prophet, cf. 58:2). It may be that this is a reference to the revelation of Yahweh's will in the preaching of the Levitical-prophetic party itself. But to understand the mercy involved, we must realize that God and his will cannot be known unless he reveals himself (cf. 55:6). There is no way, according to the Bible, that man by searching can find out God. Unless God takes the first step and draws near to man, God remains hidden and unknowable. Biblical religion is always revealed religion, dependent on God's prevenient mercy. But, Yahweh says here, he was ready to be found, ready to reveal his guiding Word, even though the Judeans were not seeking him in their worship and were not interested in his guidance (cf. Ps. 81:11. Paul uses this passage in a totally different manner in Rom. 10:20 to refer to the Gentiles.)

Yahweh continually called out "Here am I, here am I" (cf. 52:6; 58:9), which is a word play on the name "Yahweh" (cf. Exod. 3:13-15) : Yahweh is the one who is "with" Israel according to northern tradition; that is his name—"he who is with you"— and the parallelism with "name" in 1d emphasizes the point (cf. 64:7a).

< *2-5* > We even have the poignant picture of Yahweh holding out suppliant arms to his people, like a Father calling his children to return to him, v 2 (cf. 63:8; Rom. 10:21). The depth of mercy involved in such pleading is revealed in the description of the "backsliding" (cf. 57:17) that follows in the participial phrases of vv 2-5. All of the participles define the nature of the "people" in v 2b. They have continually walked in their own way rather than according to Yahweh's commandments (cf. 56:11; 57:18; 58:13; 59:8; Ps. 81:13). They have provoked (a Deuteronomic

term, cf. Deut. 4:25; Jer. 7:18; 11:17) Yahweh before his face, that
is, in worship (cf. Exod. 28:29f.; Lev. 24:3, 4, 8), by their idolatrous practices. The "gardens" of v 3c are Canaanite high places
(cf. 1:29). "Bricks" probably refers to brickwork altars, though
some would emend the phrase to read "upon the mountains" as
in v 7c. Nights spent in tombs, v 4, refers to forbidden cults of the
dead, while v 4b is a reference to pagan incubation rites. The law
of Lev. 11:7 prohibited the eating of swine's flesh, v 4c, because
the pig was a Canaanite totem animal; and broth made from such
forbidden animals was considered unclean, v 4d.

Finally, in v 5, we have a reference to the supposed holiness of
the Zadokite priests, who were set apart to the service of the altar
and forbidden therefore to touch anything unholy, that is, anything or anyone in the secular sphere and therefore unclean and
contaminating (cf. Ezek. 44:5, 13, 15; it is for this reason that the
priest and Levite "pass by on the other side" in the story of the
Good Samaritan, Luke 10:31-32; cf. Isa. 58:7. Paul Hanson, pp.
148ff., has conclusively shown that this is the meaning of v 5).
Such Zadokites have presumed to be set apart to Yahweh's service
in an exclusivity that overlooks the idolatrous worship and unjust
social practices taking place in the community.

Yet to all such persons, Yahweh has held out hands of loving
supplication, begging them to return to him—and they have not.
This then is sin "with a high hand" (cf. Num. 15:30), sin flaunted
before the very Presence of God himself like a fist shaken in his
face. That sin, the Bible maintains, cannot be forgiven (cf. Mark
3:28-30). In a stunning contrast to the Zadokite claims to holiness,
v 5cd states that the Zadokites and their idolatrous followers are
instead accursed, kindling the smoke and fire of Yahweh's con-
suming wrath (cf. Jer. 17:4; Deut. 32:22). Prayers for such rebels
are in vain. They must be destroyed.

< 6-7 >   The sentence upon them is therefore pronounced. So
certain is the judgment that it is like words written on a scroll
and read by Yahweh. In answer to the question in 64:12 in the

lament, Yahweh replies that he will by no means keep silent (cf. 57:11; 42:14; Ps. 50:3, 21). Rather he will repay (cf. 58:18; 61:8; 62:11; Jer. 16:18) the iniquity of the rebels (cf. 13:11; 22:14; 26:21) and of their fathers alike (cf. Ezek. 20:27-28). (6c is a dittography from v 7f and should be eliminated). The sin of the fathers is included, because nothing has been learned from the exile. Iniquity is heaped up (contra Ezek. 18) and now overflows in continued baalistic worship (cf. Hos. 2:13), in deliberate defiance of Yahweh. Yahweh will therefore carefully measure out (cf. Jer. 13:25; 32:18; Ruth 3:15) the judgment which the rebels have earned, bringing it upon their heads and repaying it into their bosoms (cf. Ps. 79:12), that is, into their hearts, so that the punishment engulfs the sinners' persons, externally and internally alike. The Divine Warrior not only destroys his enemies among the foreign nations (cf. 63:1-6). He also will destroy his enemies within his covenant community. Such is the only devastating result possible when God's forgiving mercy is rejected.

The question that arises in connection with such a conclusion, however, is that age-old query of Abraham's: "Wilt thou indeed destroy the righteous with the wicked?" There are yet faithful followers of Yahweh within the Judean community—those who have walked in his ways and who have sought him with a contrite heart and humble spirit. But humanity is bound together in communities of the good and the evil, "the wheat and the tares (weeds)" together (Matt. 13:24-30). Will then the wheat be uprooted along with the weeds? Are we so united with one another, so involved in one another's lives, that we are accomplices in the community's evil? Some in modern-day America have argued that we are; and in a profound sense, we each are responsible for our neighbor's sin. If we are our "brother's keeper" (Gen. 4:9), we share also his guilt. It is a dilemma with which the Bible wrestles throughout its pages (cf. Hab. 1; Jer. 31:29; Ezek. 18; Matt. 13:24-30; John 9:2)—that a God of justice should destroy the good with the evil (cf. Gen. 18:25)—and it is with this dilemma that the following portions of Trito-Isaiah deal.

Isaiah 65:8-25

8   Thus says Yahweh: Just as
    new wine is found in the cluster
    and one says, "Do not destroy it
    for there is a blessing in it;"
    so I will do for the sake of my servants
    [and] not destroy the whole.

9   But I will bring forth from Jacob a seed (descendants),
    and from Judah an inheritor of my mountains;
    and my chosen ones shall inherit it,
    and my servants shall dwell there.

10 And Sharon shall become a rest for sheep
    and the Valley of Achor a place for cattle to lie down,
    for my people who seek me.

                        ———

11 But you, who forsake Yahweh,
    who forget my holy mountain,
    who prepare a table for Gad,
    and who fill up [cups] for a drink-offering to Meni,

12 I will offer you up to Cherebh (Sword),
    and all of you shall bow down to Tebhach (Slaughter),
    because I called and you did not answer;
    I spoke and you did not listen;
    and you did that which is evil in my eyes,
    and those things in which I do not delight, you chose.

                        ———

13 Therefore, thus says
    the Lord Yahweh:
    Behold! my servants shall eat,
    but you shall suffer hunger.
    Behold! my servants shall drink,
    but you shall thirst.
    Behold! my servants shall rejoice,
    but you shall be ashamed.

14 Behold! my servants shall shout with joy
    from a good heart,

but you shall cry out from pain of heart,
and from a breaking spirit you shall wail.
15   And you shall leave your name
for a curse for my chosen ones:
"May the Lord Yahweh slay you!"

But his servants he will name
by another name,
16   so that the one who blesses himself in the land will bless
himself
by the true God;
and the one who swears in the land shall swear
by the true God;
for the former troubles will be forgotten,
and they will be hid from my eyes.
17   For behold! I am creating
new heavens
and a new earth;
and the former things shall not be remembered,
and they shall not be put to heart (come to mind).
18   So rejoice
and be glad forever
over what I am creating.

For behold! I am creating
Jerusalem an exultation
and her people a rejoicing.
19   And I will be glad (exult) over Jerusalem,
and I will rejoice over my people;
and there will not be heard in her again
a voice of weeping
and a voice of bitter crying.
20   There shall not be there again
an infant [who lives only a few] days
or an old man who does not complete
his life. For the child

will not die for a hundred years,
    but the sinner will be cursed for a hundred years.
21 They shall build houses and dwell [in them];
    and they shall plant vineyards
    and eat their fruit.
22 They shall not build and another dwell;
    they shall not plant and another eat;
    for as the days of the tree shall be the days of my people,
    and the works of their hands
    shall my chosen ones enjoy.
23 They shall not labor in vain,
    and they shall not bear children [only to have them]
        suddenly destroyed;
    for a seed blessed
    by Yahweh are they,
    and their children with them.
24 And it shall come to pass [that] before they call,
    I will answer;
    while they are still speaking,
    I will hear.

———

25 Wolf and lamb shall pasture together,
    and lion shall eat straw like an ox,
    and dust will be the serpent's bread.
  They shall not destroy and they shall not lay waste
    in all my holy mountain,
    says Yahweh.

This salvation-judgment oracle is intimately connected with the judgment oracle in 65:1-7 and should be read along with it, despite the fact that 65:1-7 are a complete form in themselves. Here we have the answer to the question of whether or not Yahweh will destroy the faithful in Judah along with the unfaithful. For the first time in the Old Testament, we find Yahweh acting in an ultimate manner toward Israel in two different ways. To the faithful he will give final salvation; to the unfaithful, death. The people of Israel is now dissolved into two separate groups with two separate destinies. The community of the nation is broken in a manner never again healed.

There were preparations for this separation between the faithful and unfaithful in what went before. Isaiah's (1:9; 10:20-23) and Zephaniah's (3:11-13) preaching about a remnant envisioned the remainder or return of the faithful few (cf. Jer. 24:4-7). Ezekiel spelled out in careful detail the possibility of life in the mercy of God for those individuals who turned from their evil ways (Ezek. 18; 33). And yet, when those prophets dealt with God's final future, they spoke of that future in relation to Israel as a people, and they envisioned the covenant community retaining its wholeness as the elect of God (cf. Isa. 2:2-4; Ezek. 37; Jer. 31:31-34, and the interpretation given to Zephaniah's words in the addition of 3:14-20). Paul stands in this prophetic tradition when he writes of "all Israel" in Rom. 11:26.

Here now in Third Isaiah, however, the former covenant community is no more, and the relationship with God is no longer mediated solely through that community. Rather, we have the equivalent in 65:8-25 of a new election by Yahweh, replacing the first election at the exodus. Second Isaiah had seen the deliverance from Babylonian captivity as a recapitulation and completion of the first exodus event (cf. 43:14-21; 52:11-12; 51:9-11), but Trito-Isaiah reinterprets that view in a totally new way. The election now has nothing to do with the deliverance from Egypt; the old exodus traditions are not even used. Yahweh forms a new chosen group for himself quite apart from the exodus remembrance.

Perhaps the prophetic struggle with evil and idolatry and injustice within the Israelite community had spanned so many centuries and had borne so little fruit that the Levitical-prophetic authors of Trito-Isaiah found it impossble to answer the question about the fate of the faithful in any other way. Certainly the answer they gave influenced all of the Judaic-Christian writings that came after them. Thus this particular passage is of the greatest importance in the development of the Bible's literature.

< 8-10 > The first strophe in this oracle sets forth Yahweh's new elective act, using the familiar Old Testament figure of Israel as a bunch of grapes (cf. 5:1-7). First fruits of Israel were holy (that is, set apart) to Yahweh (cf. Jer. 2:3) and offered back to him in recognition of his authorship and lordship over all life (cf. Exod. 23:19). The life in them was a sign of Yahweh's blessing, of his gift to his people. And yet the popular proverb quoted in v 8 recognizes that the first clusters found on a grapevine were not very good grapes for wine-making. Nevertheless, all of the first grapes were not destroyed, but some of them were preserved and given as first-fruit offerings, because they were signs of Yahweh's gift of life and blessing. The saying, "Do not destroy" probably even formed the title of a song sung at the grape-harvest (cf. the superscriptions to Pss. 57-59). The community of Judah is compared to these new grapes, and the promise of Yahweh is that he will not destroy them all in the judgment announced in 65:1-7, but will preserve some of them as those who are blessed (cf. 61:9).

Those to be preserved are called Yahweh's "servants" (cf. 63:17), his "chosen ones," a "seed" from Judah, and it is very clear who they are. They are the faithful Levitical-prophetic party and their followers, as in all the preceding oracles, who truly "seek Yahweh" (cf. 58:9), who are lowly and contrite in spirit (57:15), who walk in Yahweh's ways, according to his order, and who do justice and mercy to their fellows. They will inherit Zion and possess the land, v 9 (cf. 57:13), and this possession is spelled out in Deuteronomic terms as an inheritance of "rest" (cf. 63:14; 58:12; 32:18). Moreover, they will not only inherit Zion, but the whole land from the Plain of Sharon along the northwest coast to the Valley of Achor at the northwest corner of the Dead Sea, east of Jerusalem, v 10. Deuteronomy and the Deuteronomic historian always envisioned God's final gift of abundant life to his people as a gift of rest in the land, and that fulfillment is here pictured given to the faithful.

The main point to note, however, is that such salvation is the

gift of Yahweh. Just as new grapes come forth only by his gift
of life, so the faithful will have life only because Yahweh will
give it. He "will do," he "will bring forth," he will make the
faithful "his chosen ones." The entire oracle emphasizes, by its
verbs, that Yahweh's is the decisive action (cf. the discussion of
63:1-6). Only because Yahweh will choose the faithful will they
be his chosen ones." A new election of a new chosen group now
takes place, in contrast to the offer of the land to all of Judah in
60:21 and 61:7. Many of the Judeans, in their faithlessness, rejected
Yahweh's earlier gracious offer. The land therefore now will be
given only to those who seek Yahweh. They only now will be
"the sheep of his pasture" (Ps. 100:3; "sheep," "cattle," and "people" are parallel synonyms in 65:10).

< 11-15 > In contrast, the judgment oracle of this second
strophe pronounces doom on the idolators of whom we heard so
much in chs. 57-59 and in 65:1-7, namely the Zadokite priestly
party and their followers. In addition to the idolatrous practices
mentioned in 65:3-5, we are told here that they also offer sacrifices ("prepare a table") and drink-offerings to two foreign gods,
Gad and Meni. These two gods are otherwise unknown to us, but
are probably equivalent to gods of fate and fortune (cf. our contemporary fascination with astrology). In a fine play on the figure
of speech, Yahweh therefore says (v 12) that he too will make a
sacrifice—of the idolators to Sword and to Slaughter, here per-
sonified as foreign gods: "to bow down" in v 12b means to kneel
down for execution. And the charge of 65:1—that the idolators
refused to heed Yahweh's pleadings to them—is repeated in v 12cd
(cf. 41:28; 50:2). The language of 12c is Deuteronomic (cf. Jer.
7:13) and the four lines of 12c-f are repeated in 66:4, probably an
indication that the charge was a Deuteronomic formula for sin.

< 13-15a > In this third strophe, which is framed by the divine
title "the Lord Yahweh," we see how decisive has become the
split in the community. The only other places in the Old Testa-

ment where we have such lists of blessings for the faithful and curses for the unfaithful are in those lists of covenant blessings and curses connected with the making or renewal of the Sinai covenant (cf. Deut. 27-28; Lev. 26); and the fact that we find them here also reinforces the view that Trito-Isaiah here pictures a new election of a new group within Israel. As before, the title of "servants" is intended to appropriate for the Levitical-prophetic community the role of Second Isaiah's Servant. They have become the ones whom Yahweh will exalt and lift up, so that they prosper (52:13). Once again the connection with the Beatitudes should be noted ("Blessed are those who hunger . . . thirst . . . mourn . . .").

The last line of v 14 is ironic: because the unfaithful would not seek Yahweh with a broken spirit and a contrite heart (57:15), Yahweh himself will break their spirit (cf. Matt. 8:12). Further, as a covenant curse (cf. Deut. 28:37), the very name of the unfaithful will be used for a curse, that is, "May the Lord Yahweh slay you as he did so and so" (cf. Jer. 24:9; 25:18; 29:22; Zech. 8:13).

< 15b-18c >   In contrast, according to this fourth strophe, Yahweh's servants will be given a new name (cf. 56:5; 58:12; 61:3, 6; 62:2, 4). Earlier the new name was offered to the community as a whole; now it becomes the appellation of Yahweh's servants alone. But a new name implies a new character, a change in one's very being, and that is the emphasis here. The new name Yahweh gives his servants so transforms their lives that they will no longer even be tempted by idolatry. Instead they will swear only by the true God, and bless themselves only by his name. Indeed, the former troubles—that is, the idolatry and the injustices practiced by the unfaithful—will be totally done way and forgotten. Evil will be no more.

This thoroughgoing transformation is characterized in v 17 as Yahweh's creation of new heavens and a new earth. Once again this is a prophecy totally new in Old Testament history, and the verse has caused much debate. Is this the beginning of apocalypticism in the prophetic movement? That is, has the present age come to be seen as so evil that Yahweh can only do away with it by a totally new creation? Or is this simply a metaphor for Yahweh's thoroughgoing transformation of Israel's continuing history? Is there a total break here with the Israelite history of the past and the creation of a new realm? Or is there continuity with what has gone before? Certainly New Testament apocalyptic literature picked up this announcement and used it to signify a totally new age (cf. 2 Peter 3:11-13; Rev. 21:1), but the question is, how did Trito-Isaiah understand this prophecy?

Three facts militate against an apocalyptic understanding of this verse. First, the verb in vv 17 and 18 is a participle, signifying that Yahweh is already beginning his new creation and that it is a continuous process within Israel's historical life. Second, v 17d uses Second Isaiah's term, "the former things" (cf. 41:22; 42:9; 43:9, 18; 46:9), which refers to Yahweh's past saving deeds within Israel's historical existence. Third, what follows in v 18d-f immediately returns to Jerusalem's concrete setting.

To be sure, "the former things" here refer to "the former troubles," as in v 16e, and Trito-Isaiah has changed Deutero-Isaiah's meaning, as it so often does; but the word points to a continuity with the past. It cannot be denied that Trito-Isaiah says nothing about how this transformation of history will come about. Gone are any connections with the historical movements of nations. Yahweh alone is the actor on the scene. The new era of salvation comes solely by his creative power. Nevertheless, what follows in the oracle deals with Jerusalem and houses and gardens and childbirth and prayer, and the Levitical-prophetic community is looking forward to a transformation that will take place within the sphere of its historical circumstances. The door to apocalypticism has been opened only a crack here, though later writers seized upon this passage to fling the door wide open.

< *18d-20* > This fifth strophe pictures the transformation of

the life of the faithful in the concrete terms of life in a transformed Jerusalem. "My people" in v 19b now refers only to the
faithful who have been elected by Yahweh (cf. v 22c and e). The
promise of v 19c-e may be intended as a contrast to Jer. 7:34; 16:9;
and 25:10 (cf. their later apocalyptic use in Rev. 21:4). Verse 20
is a reflection of the Hebrew belief that long life was a gift of
God (cf. Deut. 4:40; Job 5:26), who is the Source of all life. Death
was a natural part of life for the Hebrew, accepted rather peace-
fully, unless it was premature or violent; then it was understood
as a judgment or curse from God. Further, as in v 20f, life could
be so uncertain under the curse of God that it was considered a
living death (cf. Deut. 28:66).

< 21-24 >   The sixth strophe reiterates much that has gone be-
fore, but the repetition of v 21 in a negative form in v 22 emphasizes how important for the writers was this promise of houses
and vineyards (cf. 62:8-9; Jer. 31:5; Amos 9:14). The figure of
the tree in 22c is a frequent one in the Old Testament (cf. 61:3;
Jer. 17:8; Ps. 92:12-14; Job 14:7-9) and suggested permanency to
the Hebrew mind. Moreover there is great appreciation for the
meaningfulness given to life by reaping the fruits of one's own
labor (v 22d and 23ab; cf. 55:2; Ps. 90:17). One of the curses on
Adam for his disobedience in the garden in Gen. 3:17-19 was
that he would not reap a reward from the ground commensurate
with his toil. Wherever labor or life took on futility, there the
Old Testament saw a cursed existence (cf. Deut. 28:30-31). We
were created by God for meaningful labor and commensurate
reward for that labor, but we have those gifts only in faithfulness
to God. Those who are faithful shall reap the reward of Yahweh's
blessings, v 23c-e (cf. Deut. 28:3-12; Isa. 61:9), and such blessing
will be extended even to their children(cf. 59:21; Jer. 32:38-41;
Acts 2:39). Above all, Yahweh will be with them, v 24, answering
them even before they pray (cf. 55:6) and hearing their petitions
even before they are finished speaking (cf. 58:9; 65:1, 12; Ps.
139:4). Finally the nearness of Yahweh to his elected ones is their

greatest good, and as such, the essential content of what the Old
Testament means by salvation. In times of trouble, then, when all
else was gone, the Old Testament person of faith held fast to the
relationship with God (cf. Hab. 3:17-18; Ps. 73; 46, etc.), and in
that relationship, as here in Trito-Isaiah, found hope for the future.

< 25 > Verse 24 contains the same motif as 65:1 and thereby
indicates that ch. 65 now forms a unity. Verse 25 is therefore an
addition to the chapter, very similar to wording found in Isa.
11:6a, 7c, and 9 ab. While the verse seems appropriate here, it
probably belonged originally to Isa. 11. The figure of the serpent
condemned to eat dust is found in Gen. 3:14 and Mic. 7:17. The
closing formula, "says Yahweh," probably originally stood at the
end of v 24.

That which should be emphasized from this whole chapter is
that the saved elect do not earn their salvation. We see here the
way the Bible understands the relationship of faith to works. It is
not because the Levitical-prophetic party and their followers do
good deeds that they will be chosen and saved from Yahweh's
judgment. In 64:6-7 they acknowledged their oneness in sin with
the whole Judean community. Rather, it is because they trust
Yahweh, because they place themselves in his merciful hands, and
do not rely on their own works or worship or inner rectitude to
guarantee their lives. The Zadokite priestly party and their followers believe that a proper cult in the center of a carefully
planned community will guarantee Yahweh's favor toward them
(cf. Ezek. 40-48). The authors of Trito-Isaiah know that abundant life comes solely as the gift of God. Here, in faith, they look
forward to the receipt of that life.

Isaiah 66:1-2, 3-4, 5-6, 7-9, 10-13, 14-18a

Isaiah 66:1-18a is made up of a number of rather brief oracles,
which probably were originally independent proclamations, delivered by various prophetic members of the Levitical-prophetic

party, but which now have been joined together to form a summary of the message of Trito-Isaiah. As in ch. 65, the proclamations alternate between judgment and salvation, and they should be read in intimate connection with one another, in the order in which they now stand. They add little new to the theology of Trito-Isaiah, but they utilize new and powerful figures of speech, which are evidence of the continuing vitality of the Leviticalprophetic community. They probably stand in the proper place in Trito-Isaiah, as representatives of the latest preaching of that community.

1   Thus says Yahweh:
     The heavens are my throne,
     and the earth a footstool for my feet.
    What is this house
     that you would build for me,
     and where is a place where I might rest?
2   All these things my hand has made,
     and they are mine—all these!
     Oracle of Yahweh.
    But this is the one to whom I will look—
     to the humble and broken in spirit,
     who trembles at my word.

---

3   Slaughtering the ox; slaying a man;
     sacrificing the sheep; breaking the neck of a dog;
    going up to make a cereal offering; bringing swine's blood;
     remembering frankincense; blessing vanity;
    yea, they choose their own ways,
     and in their abominations they delight.

---

4   Yea, I will choose their misfortunes,
     and I will bring what they fear upon them;
    because I called and there was no answer;
     I spoke and they did not hear;

but they did the evil in my eyes,
and what I do not delight in, they chose.

5　Hear the word of Yahweh,
　　you who tremble at his word:
　　Your brothers who hate you,
　　and who cast you out for the sake of my name, say,
　　"Let Yahweh be glorified,
　　and let us see your joy!"
　　But they shall be ashamed.

6　A sound of tumult from the city!
　　A sound from the temple!
　　A sound of Yahweh recompensing
　　[their] reward to his enemies!

7　Before she travailed,
　　she gave birth;
　　before her pain came,
　　she was delivered of a son.
8　Who has heard of anything like this?
　　Who has seen things like these?
　　Shall a land be brought forth
　　in one day?
　　Shall a people be born
　　in one moment?
　　For as soon as Zion was in labor
　　she brought forth her sons.
9　Shall I break the water-bag (lit: womb) and not bring forth?
　　says Yahweh.
　　Shall I, who brings forth, not [also] complete (lit: close)?
　　says your God.

---

10   Rejoice with Jerusalem, and be glad in her,
        all you who love her!
        Be joyful over her joy,
        all you who mourn over her!
11   That you may suck and be satisfied
        [with] your comfort from [her] breast,
        that you may suck fully and enjoy yourself
        from the abundance of her glory.
12   For thus says Yahweh:
        Behold, I am extending to her
        abundant life (Hebr.: shalom) like a river,
        and like an overflowing stream,
        the glory of the nations.
        And you shall suck. You shall be carried upon the hip,
        and upon the knees you shall be dandled.
13   Like a son whose mother comforts him,
        so will I comfort you,
        and in Jerusalem you shall be comforted.

14   You shall see and your heart will rejoice,
        and your bones will flourish like fresh grass,
        and it shall be known that the hand of Yahweh is with his
                servants,
        but wrath upon his enemies.
15   For behold! Yahweh
        comes like a fire,
        and like a whirlwind are his war chariots,
        to render his anger in fury
        and his rebuke in the flames of fire.
16   For with fire Yahweh will execute judgment,
        and with his sword, [against] all flesh,
        and those slain by Yahweh will be many.
17   Those who set themselves apart and those who purify
                themselves [to go into] the gardens,
        one after the other (?),

eating the flesh of the swine
and [of] the defiled thing and [of] the mouse,
together they shall perish, oracle of Yahweh,
18   for [I know] their works and their thoughts.

< 1-2 > The first oracle is a prophetic torah or teaching con-
cerning the efforts of the Zadokite party to rebuild the temple.
Such efforts are vividly pictured in the prophecies of Haggai (520
B.C.) and First Zechariah (520-518 B.C.; cf. Ezra 4:24—6:18), and
this oracle may date from about their time. It sets forth the northern prophetic protest against imprisoning the Ruler of the universe in a house made by human hands, a protest that was present
in Israel from very early times (cf. 2 Sam. 7:4-7). Yahweh is a
God who is on the move, according to the Old Testament. He is
a God who goes with his people during the wilderness wanderings, enthroned above his portable shrine, the ark (cf. Exod.
33:16; Num. 10:33-36). He can be in Babylonia as easily as in
Palestine (cf. Jer. 29:7; Ezek. 1). He does not confine himself to
a temple, but only places his name there (cf. Deut. 12:11 et passim) that he may be worshiped by his people. And, as here, he
destroys all efforts to domesticate him within a house or cult (cf.
Jer. 7:1-15).

As in Second Isaiah (cf. 40:12-31), God is enthroned above the
universe in the picture of this oracle (cf. Ps. 11:4), the earth a
mere footstool for his feet (cf. Matt. 5:34-35; Acts 7:49-50). So
he waves his hand out across his universe and says, "All of this is
mine, because I fashioned it (cf. Ps. 24:1-2). Are you going to
confine me, then, within a tiny temple?" There is very much a
feeling of Yahweh's immensity here, of the vast spaces it would
take to encompass him (cf. 1 Kings 8:27; Jer. 23:23)—a note felt
also in First Isaiah (cf. the way Yahweh "fills" all in Isa. 6:1-12),
and a note which we, with our modern understandings of the
vastness of space, may appreciate all the more.

In view of the fact that the Levites wish to serve as priests in the temple on Zion, this protest against the rebuilding of the temple may seem surprising, and it is questionable if this oracle is intended to reject the temple as such. Rather, it is a protest against the Zadokites' misunderstanding of the function of the temple as a *guarantee* of Yahweh's presence in the midst of his people. Nothing can guarantee God. No one can manipulate him or command his will and Presence (cf. 40:13-14). If he dwells with his people, he does so out of his own free choice and gracious condescendence, and the final lines of his oracle tell with whom Yahweh will dwell. As earlier in Trito-Isaiah (cf. 57:15), he promises that he will "look to," that is, hear the prayers, accept the worship, and draw near to those who humbly approach him in repentance and trust (cf. Ps. 34:18; Matt. 5:3; Luke 18:13-14). Then a new description is given of the faithful: they are those who "tremble at" or "revere" Yahweh's Word (cf. Ezra 9:4; 10:3). The phrase probably refers to obedience to the Deuteronomic law and especially to its stipulations against idolatry. No temple worship is acceptable, the oracle is saying, which is not carried out in pure and sincere trust in Yahweh alone (cf. John 4:20-21).

< *3-4* > In this judgment oracle, such true worship is then contrasted with that of the Zadokites and their followers. Contrary to those commentators who consider v 3 to be a series of wisdom-like similes and who add a phrase to each line to form a comparison (e.g., "Slaughtering the ox is like slaying a man"), v 3 is simply a listing of the worship practices of the Zadokite party. They offer the legitimate burnt and cereal offerings (Lev. 2:1-2 connects frankincense with the cereal offering), and such sacrifices would be quite acceptable to Yahweh if offered in true fidelity to him. But the difficulty is that the Zadokite party also offers heathen sacrifices to heathen gods. They engage in child sacrifice (the Hebrew *'ish* is used to refer to a male child also in vv 7d and 13a; for the practice, cf. 57:5). They eat the flesh of dogs, offered

to the gods.[1] They bring the blood of the unclean swine to Yahweh's altar (cf. 65:4). They bless, that is, they honor and worship
"vanity," which is a term Second Isaiah uses to describe the emptiness and inability of foreign idols to work in history (41:29).
Moreover, the Zadokite party engages in such idolatry by free
choice. They "choose" to walk in their own ways rather than in
Yahweh's way—a motif found throughout Trito-Isaiah (cf. 56:11;
57:10, 17, 18; 58:13; 59:7, 8; 65:2)—and they take delight in their
heathen rituals (cf. 57:8; 58:2, 13; 65:12), a phrase which indicates
not only superficial pleasure but also the love within the Zadokites'
hearts.

Therefore, over-against the choice which the Zadokite party
makes, Yahweh will also make a choice, v 4. They choose the gods
of fate and fortune (cf. 65:11), but the future is in Yahweh's
hands, and by his choice the outcome of such idolatry will be
misfortunes (cf. 65:11). The Zadokite party worships out of fear
rather than out of love, and it tries to placate the gods and to
manipulate them into bringing favor upon Judah. Therefore the
very destruction that the Zadokite party dreads will be brought
upon it.

Lines c-f of v 4 repeat the words of 65:12 and probably originally belonged there, but have been added here because of the
reoccurrence of the key word "chose" in line f. Certainly lines
4ab would form a suitable ending to this judgment oracle, which
once again hammers home the proclamation of the freedom of
God. As Yahweh is never bound to the temple, vv 1-2, so here he
is never coerced by ritual, and sacrifices are never automatically
efficacious. They must be offered in trust and not fear, in obedience and not rebellion, in love for Yahweh alone, who holds the
future in his hands. Trito-Isaiah is concerned with freedom here
—the freedom of a sovereign God—and the freedom of worshipers from fear and anxious ritualism when they truly love God.

---

1. Muilenburg states in *The Interpreter's Bible,* Vol. V, p. 762: "According to
Justin, *History of the World,* XIX.1.10, Darius forbade the Carthaginians to
offer human victims in sacrifice or to eat the flesh of dogs."

We do not try to placate the Lord if we worship truly; rather we respond in heartfelt love and trust to the love he has poured out upon us, offering our lives and goods in the service of his purpose. Such offering alone, Trito-Isaiah says, is pleasing to God. He delights in human beings who freely come in love to worship him.

< 5-6> The third oracle is a combination of judgment and salvation, but it is spoken to the faithful Levitical-prophetic party, who "tremble at" or obey Yahweh's Word in the Deuteronomic law (cf. 2f), and it therefore offers comfort to them in the form of judgment on their enemies. The enemies are specifically described as "your brothers who hate you and who cast you out for the sake of my name" (cf. Ps. 38:20; Matt. 5:10-12; 10:22; John 15:18-20). The reference can be to no other than the Zadokite priests who have excluded the Levites from service at Yahweh's altar because of the Levites' supposed idolatry (cf. the polemic in Ezek. 44:10), and who have subjected the Levites to scorn (cf. 57:4; 58:9), to segregation (cf. 63:16; 65:5), and even to death (cf. 57:1-2). This is the only time Trito-Isaiah calls the Zadokites "brothers" of the Levites, and the term refers to membership in Israel (cf. Deut. 1:16; 2:4; 3:18; Jer. 7:15; 29:16). This is also the only time Trito-Isaiah describes the Zadokites' attitude toward the Levites as hatred, though we have seen ample evidence throughout the book that the description is accurate.

In v 5ef, the reference is to the project of rebuilding the temple. "Let Yahweh be glorified by rebuilding his temple," the Zadokites are saying, "and then, you Levites, rejoice over the building and thank God that it has been restored!" (cf. Hag. 1:8; Zech. 2:10). In other words, the Zadokites are telling the Levites to amend their attitude toward the temple project and to acquiesce in its restoration. However, the judgment of Yahweh in 5g is that the Zadokites will be shamed (cf. Luke 13:17) and their efforts brought to naught.

The second strophe of the oracle, v 6, then sets forth in a vivid metaphor, Yahweh's actual future judgment upon the Zadokites:

a commotion is heard by the Levites, here pictured as standing at a distance outside Jerusalem. As they run into the city, they discover that the tumult is coming from the temple (cf. Rev. 16:1, 17). When they hurry to the temple, they see the cause of the cries and noise: Yahweh is there in the future, rebuilt temple, bringing the consequences of the Zadokites' idolatry and superstition upon them (cf. 59:18; 65:6f.; 35:4; Joel 3:7). The passage does not yet say what form Yahweh takes or what his reward (cf. 3:11) is for his enemies. Those are spelled out later in the chapter.

< 7-9 >   Instead, there stands at this point a salvation oracle to the Levitical-prophetic party and its followers, and it has much the same theme as had 65:8-10, 13-25: Yahweh will create a new elect people, a new "son" for himself (cf. the former Israel as son of Yahweh in Hos. 11:1; Isa. 1:2; Exod. 4:22-23; Deut. 8:5; Jer. 31:20) from the faithful in Judah and Jerusalem, specifically from the Isaianic and Jeremianic prophets, from the Levites, and from their followers. The messaage is announced in the form of an extended metaphor, in which Jerusalem is pictured as a woman (cf. 60:1) giving birth to a male child (cf. 49:20-21; Rev. 12:5). But the suddenness and imminence of the birth are emphasized. Even before her birth pangs start—which, allegorically, might refer to Jerusalem's trials after 538 B.C.—she brings forth a son. That is, before Jerusalem is in real distress, the new covenant people of Yahweh will be born.

The amazing nature of this act that Yahweh will accomplish is set forth in the astonished questions of an unidentified speaker in v 8 (cf. 64:4), a style very much like that of Second Isaiah in 40:12ff. and of Jeremiah in 2:11; 8:4ff. and elsewhere. Yahweh is actually going to create a new people for himself in one day— nay, in one moment. The act of making a new covenant people can therefore only be Yahweh's act (cf. the emphasis on the absence of all help for Yahweh in 63:1-6), and once again the futility of the Zadokites' efforts to create a restored and ideal people is being emphasized. It reminds one of the new people of

the Christian church, born in a moment on the day of Pentecost
(Acts 2).

Yahweh then asks his own questions, in v 9. Should he begin
an action and not complete it? His salvation of his people has
been started: they have returned from exile, been brought back
to their own land, in fulfillment of the prophets' promises. Yahweh's Word has stood, and come to pass, as Second Isaiah said it
would (40:8; 55:10-11). Will he not then also give them that
future abundant life promised by the prophets? Will he not exalt
his servants, as he said he would (cf. 52:13)?—and we must remember that in Trito-Isaiah, the Levitical-prophetic party and
their followers have taken over the role of the Suffering Servant.
Will Yahweh not create the new covenant people, promised in his
past Word? (Note the covenant phrase "your God" at the end of
v 9). Of course he will! It is inconceivable that Yahweh should
not fulfill his Word, that he should start a saving action and not
bring it to completion (cf. 37:3 for the figure of speech). Verse 9
is intended as certain comfort for the faithful, who perhaps cannot
see any hope for themselves beyond their immediate sufferings,
who may have lost sight of the coming light (cf. 60:1) in the
midst of their present darkness, who perhaps despair of any fruit-
ful outcome of their faithfulness to their God. God will complete
his good work in them. That has been the firm ground of hope
for the faithful in every generation (cf. Phil. 1:6).

< 10-13 >   This salvation oracle therefore addresses the faithful
"who love Jerusalem" (cf. Ps. 26:8; 122:6; 137:6), by which is
meant those who love the God of Jerusalem and who hold fast to
his plans for her. They are also addressed as those "who have
mourned over" Jerusalem (cf. 60:20; 61:2f.), namely over her
desperate and sinful state. Now such faithful lovers of Yahweh
and of his holy hill are called to rejoice over the gladness which
Yahweh is going to bring to his sacred city, in order that they
may share in the consolations which she will experience. Yahweh
is going to keep his Word of comfort, promised in Isa. 40:1 and

49:13. He is going to comfort Jerusalem. And from her comfort, all those who love Jerusalem will be able to draw comfort. As in ch. 60:4ff., Jerusalem is pictured as a mother, and when she is consoled, all her faithful children will be able to nurse fully and deeply at her overflowing breast (cf. 60:16), which is described here as her "glory" (cf. 60:2, 9, 19; 62:2). Yahweh will cause abundant life *(shalom)* to flow out upon Jerusalem like a river: lines 12bc quote 48:18, and we see from that latter passage that Yahweh has long desired to give Jerusalem such life.

Further, the "glory," that is, the wealth, of the nations will flow to Zion like an overflowing stream (cf. 60:5ff., 11, 13; 61:6). And from all this abundance, the faithful will be nourished, allowed to suckle at their Mother Jerusalem's breast, and to be carried on her hip (cf. 60:4) and dandled upon her knees. As a little boy is comforted by his mother, so the faithful will be comforted by Mother Jerusalem, v 13. But then we see in line b of this verse who really brings consolation and protection and love: Yahweh is acting through it all, comforting his faithful followers (cf. 12:1). He would not give comfort to the wicked (57:6d); he would not give them abundant life (57:21). But he will give these gifts to his new elect people and thus fulfill his Word (cf. 2 Cor. 1:3-5).

< 14-16 > The sixth oracle is a combination salvation-judgment oracle, much like that in 65:13ff., where we have the same contrast between the fate of the faithful and of the unfaithful. The faithful will see Yahweh's salvation of Zion, and their hearts will rejoice (cf. 60:5; 65:14). "Bones" is a synonym for their inner vitality (cf. 58:11; Ezek. 37:1ff.) which will become as abundant as new grass. But not only the faithful will "see," according to v 14; a universal revelation is implied (cf. 60:3, 14; 61:6, 9, 11; 62:2). "It shall be known" by all in the world that Yahweh has saved his "servants,"—the title for the faithful which was used so prominently in 65:8, 9, 13-15; cf. 63:17—and that he has lifted his hand in wrath against his enemies. The authors of Trito-Isaiah

are concerned not just for their own salvation, but for that of all peoples.

Yahweh's destruction of his enemies, previously alluded to in v 6, now is portrayed in more graphic figures, v 15, and as in 59:15c-20 and 63:1-6, the picture is of Yahweh the Divine Warrior. Line c is a quote from Jeremiah's description of the Foe from the North in Jer. 4:13, but the reference to Yahweh's war chariots also recalls Ps. 68:17 and Hab. 3:8, and the remarkable pictures in those latter two passages of Yahweh's destruction of his enemies, of his dwelling on Zion, and of his presence with his people at the exodus and in the wilderness, remind here of some of the most ancient election traditions of Israel. We are evidently dealing in this final chapter of Trito-Isaiah once again with Yahweh's choice of a new people for himself, at the same time that he destroys his enemies among his former people and among the nations of the world. The figure of fire for Yahweh's judgment is one of the most frequent in the Isaiah corpus (cf. 5:24; 9:5, 18f.; 10:16; 26:11; 30:27; 33:14; 47:14; 64:2; 65:5). We saw an earlier reference in 65:12 to the "sword" of v 16 (cf. 34:6). Yahweh the Divine Warrior comes, as we have seen so often before, with salvation for the faithful and with death for the unfaithful.

< 17-18a > These verses are considered by many to belong to the following prose section, but they really form the conclusion of the oracle in vv 14-16. We hear once again of the cultic sins of the Zadokite party—of their claim to be "set apart" as holy to Yahweh (cf. 65:5), and yet of their idolatry in heathen gardens (cf. 65:3; 1:29), their eating of swine (65:4; cf. Lev. 11:7) and of unclean or defiled animals (the reference can be to any one of a number of creatures; cf. Lev. 11:12ff.) and even of mice (cf. Lev. 11:29). Those so defiant of Yahweh's law can never be acceptable to him. "Together" (cf. 1:28, 31) they shall all die, is the judgment of God. Their ways are not hidden from him. Thus, while the oracle envisions Yahweh's judgment on all flesh, and picks up the theme of 63:1-6, for example, its major concern is never-

theless with the unfaithful in Judah and specifically with those
of the Zadokite party. Their end is death. They have chosen it
(cf. v 3) for themselves.

Isaiah 66:18b-21

18 ((And)) I am coming to gather all nations and tongues.
And they shall come and they shall see my glory. 19
And I will put among them a sign. And from them I will send
survivors to the nations, [to] Tarshish, Put and Lud, Meschech and Rosh, [to] Tubal and Javan, [to] the coastlands
far off, who have not heard my fame and have not seen
my glory. And they shall declare my glory among the nations. 20 And they shall bring all your brothers from
all the nations as an offering to Yahweh, upon horses, and
in chariots, and upon litters, and upon mules, and upon
dromedaries, to my holy mountain, Jerusalem, says Yahweh, just as the children of Israel bring the cereal offering
in a clean vessel to the house of Yahweh. 21 And even
from them I will take Levitical priests, says Yahweh.

Verse 18 of this prose section is obviously corrupt, but by at-
taching part of its first phrase to v 17, and by emending the femi-
nine participle, "she is coming" to "I am coming," good sense is
restored.

The universal vision with which Trito-Isaiah began, in 56:1-8,
is recalled and broadened. In v 16, Yahweh was pictured exe-
cuting his judgment on all flesh. In v 17, his judgment fell on the
idolators of Judah. But now, after the purging fire of his judgment, he comes to gather together all remaining nations and
tongues (cf. Zech. 8:23; Dan. 3:4). Once again, the act is Yahweh's alone. And his purpose in gathering together all peoples
is to show them his glory (cf. 59:19; 60:1). The Word of Second
Isaiah will be fulfilled; all flesh will see the glory of Yahweh
(40:5).

Consonant with the earlier thought of Trito-Isaiah, this glory of God—here his material Presence on earth—will be manifested in Judah (cf. 60:1-3), when he comes to her to transform her life. This will be the "sign" for the nations, referred to in v 19— Yahweh's salvation of his people by his Presence in their midst (cf. Isa. 11:10, 12; 62:10). By this sign, all peoples will know that Yahweh is true God and Savior. Therefore, from among those in the nations who have survived Yahweh's universal judgment, there will be those willing to become missionaries, those willing to go into all the world to tell of Yahweh's saving acts and to declare his honor to all peoples ("glory" in the last phrase of v 19 has its other Old Testament meaning of "fame" or "esteem" or "honor"; cf. 42:12; 1 Chron. 16:24).

These missionaries will be sent by Yahweh to Tarshish in Spain (cf. 2:16; 60:9; Ezek. 27:12), to Put (the LXX reading) and Lud in Africa (cf. Gen. 10:6, 13; Ezek. 27:10; 30:5), to Meschech (LXX) and Rosh (LXX) and Tubal (cf. Ezek. 38:2; 39:1) in Asia Minor, to Javan in Greece (cf. Ezek. 27:13), and to the most distant coastlands—in short, throughout all the known world, to all who have not heard of Yahweh and what he has done for his new covenant people. The result will be that all nations will come to Zion (cf. 2:2-3), bringing with them the Jews who have been dispersed throughout the world (cf. 60:4, 9; 49:22; 43:6), as a glad offering to God. And what better homage could the nations render to Yahweh than to participate in his saving work by bringing back his people to his holy mountain (cf. 11:9; 56:7; 65:11, 25; 57:13)? This is true worship of God, to work the works that he works, and so the nations will join in his work of bringing his people home. So too do all Christians offer glad homage to God when they bring others into the Body of Christ, the church. The work of evangelism is an offering to God, compared here to the gift of the cereal offering.

The most daring announcement, paralleling that of 56:3-8, comes in v 21. From among the foreigners streaming to Zion, Yahweh will choose some to become Levitical priests. (In the Hebrew, "as priests" is explained by the following word, "as Le-

vites" and should not be emended with the version to read "as
priests and Levites"). Just as in 56:7, the temple is to be a house
of prayer for all nations, and eunuchs and foreigners will be accepted in it, so here too they will be accepted. But even more is
said: foreigners can be priests, offering sacrifices to God and performing the duties of the sacred altar. Such an announcement
would have been anathema to the Zadokite party, but the mercy
of God goes beyond all our thoughts and our ways, and it is because of that mercy that we Gentiles have indeed become Yahweh's "kingdom of priests" (1 Peter 2:5, 9).

Isaiah 66:22-24

22 For as the new heavens
       and the new earth
       which I am making
    shall remain before me, oracle of Yahweh,
       so shall your descendants and your name remain.
23 And it shall come to pass, every new moon
       and every sabbath,
    [that] all flesh will come to worship
       before me, says Yahweh.
24 And they shall go forth and see
       the dead bodies of the men
       who rebelled against me;
    for their worm shall not die,
       and their fire shall not be quenched,
       and they shall be an object of aversion for all flesh.

This final oracle, vv 22-24, is, appropriate to the whole of Trito-
Isaiah, a combination salvation-judgment oracle, once again in
poetry. The promise of new heavens and a new earth is picked up
from 65:17 (see) and used as the basis of Yahweh's guarantee to
the faithful. Just as the new, transformed universe will last forever and never be destroyed, so the descendants of the faithful and
the names of the faithful which they bear shall continue forever,

in generation after generation (cf. 56:5). The thought is not of eternal life for the faithful (in contrast with John 10:27-29; 1 Peter 1:4), but for the one form of immortality that the Hebrews knew at the time—namely, perpetuation of one's name and person in one's children and one's children's children (cf.. 59:21; 61:9; 65:9, 23). The community of Yahweh's new chosen people will now continue forever.

In that community will be included representatives of all peoples, and v 23 pictures their procession up Zion to worship Yahweh on the occasion of every month's festival and every week's sabbath (cf. 19:21, 23; 45:22-23). The whole world now centers in Jerusalem and pays homage to God in his temple.

But v 24 closes the book on a terrible note. As the worshipers leave the holy place, they see, on the city's refuse heap, the dead, unburied bodies of the unfaithful in Judah. The bodies are of those who have rebelled against Yahweh—the verb is the strongest prophetic term for sin, indicating high-handed defiance of God's rule (cf. 57:4; 58:1; 59:12, 13, 20)—and thus they have not only been slain but have suffered the ultimate indignity, for the Hebrew mind, of lack of proper burial. At the city's dump, their bodies feed worm (cf. 14:11; 15:8) and fire (cf. the quotation of this verse by Jesus in Mark 9:48), and they serve as a source of disgust and aversion to all true worshipers of God, not only because of their awful appearance in death but because their bodies remind of their lives of contempt for God. That the verse is intended as a final judgment on the Zadokite party cannot be doubted. At the same time, it is intended as comfort for the Levitical-prophetic party and their followers, who have suffered such scorn and persecution at the hands of the Zadokites. God's enemies will be destroyed, and his new realm will come.

Thus this book, which dreamed of a Jerusalem whose people could all be righteous (60:21); which envisioned all nations streaming out of the darkness into the light of a faithful and transformed city (60:1-3); which envisioned God's purpose fulfilled for Israel, a blessing in the midst of the earth (61:9); which longed for God's everlasting Presence with his own as Comforter and Redeemer and King (chs. 61, 62), ends with Jerusalem divided and her first covenant come to nought; with a new, elect few remaining who have known how to worship God in humility and contriteness of heart; with the necessity of new heavens and a new earth to overcome humanity's evil ways. God's purposes of bringing salvation and of establishing his kingdom on earth do not fail. His Word stands forever sure. But human beings make awful and decisive choices about their places in that coming kingdom.

It has seemed to be ever so in Jerusalem. Almost six centuries later, when God's Son rode into his holy city, he wept again over its divisions, grieving that it did not know the things that would bring it abundant life (Luke 19:41-42). And he had to cleanse his temple again and quote the words of Trito-Isaiah (Luke 19:46).

So too today, he comes surely to his people, the church. And he tells us that there will yet be a final division, in which some will enter into everlasting life and some into eternal punishment (Matt. 25:14-46). It is not an announcement we like to hear. We block it out by easily assuring ourselves that we will all be forgiven; and to be sure, 'God holds out hands of forgiving love to us in the cross and resurrection of Jesus Christ, just as he held out his hands all the day to Israel in Trito-Isaiah's time, and called out, "Here am I, here am I" (65:1-2). But we have to respond to his call in faith and humility and obedience. It is that choice of which Trito-Isaiah reminds us. It is that response to which Trito-Isaiah summons us.

O God of the prophets and of our Lord Jesus Christ: grant us through the power of thy Holy Spirit, hearts that love Thee and lives that obey Thee, that we may be found faithful servants in thy final choice and thus enter into thy eternal kingdom. Through the mercy at work in thy Son, our Lord. Amen. To thy Name be the glory.

Trito-Isaiah and the
Problem of the Canon

Trito-Isaiah raises serious problems for our understanding of the canonical authority of the Bible, for as we have seen, it contains views diametrically opposed to those of the Priestly writers, of Haggai and Zechariah, and of portions of Ezekiel. If, theologically, we accept the positions of Trito-Isaiah, must we then reject the positions represented by the Zadokite priestly party, even though the latter form the predominant view in the Old Testament canon?

How can we confess with Haggai, for example, that it was absolutely necessary for the post-exilic Jews to rebuild the temple and reinstitute the Zadokite service at the altar, and yet at the same time affirm with Trito-Isaiah that temple-building and priesthood are secondary to humble and contrite faith in God? Is a solely spiritual religion sufficient for human worship, or is there not a legitimate place for temples and ritual and ordained priesthood? Certainly Protestant churches have argued over such questions of legitimate worship forms for centuries, and denomi-

nations are often distinguished from one another by their positions on these very questions.

For that matter, how can we take at face value Trito-Isaiah's
scathing denunciations of the idolatry and unjust social practices
of the Zadokite party's followers, and at the same time trust the
integrity of the scriptural writings that the Zadokites produced?
The Zadokite priestly writers may have edited the entire corpus
of the Old Testament. Can we trust the witness of those so condemned by Trito-Isaiah?

More seriously still, it is quite evident in subsequent Jewish
history that the Zadokite party, so evil in Trito-Isaiah's eyes, was
not judged by God and destroyed, despite Trito-Isaiah's words.
The promised new heavens and earth were not created; and the
salvation announced by Trito-Isaiah did not come to Jerusalem's
faithful remnant. Have these words fallen by the wayside after
all, and was Trito-Isaiah wrong about the Word of God? Despite
the attempt by the Levitical-prophetic party to perpetuate the
message of Second Isaiah, has it now happened that the Word of
God does not stand forever, that it was not fulfilled and never
will be?

In answer to these very serious questions, we must realize that
they arise not only from a study of Trito-Isaiah, but every time
we study the Bible. The canon is shot through with contradictory
theological positions and writings produced by sinful human
beings and promises of a salvation that seemingly has never
come. Our study of Trito-Isaiah has simply brought the questions
once again to the fore. But because Trito-Isaiah is such a polemical document, it perhaps raises the questions in a clearer fashion
than do some other portions of the Scriptures.

It is not difficult to find other portions of the Old Testament,
and of the New for that matter, that have contradictory theological views. For example, one portion of 1 Samuel sees the Davidic
kingship as a gift from God, while another part views the institution of the monarchy as an act of apostasy on Israel's part. Or
Hosea and Jeremiah consider the wilderness time to have been

the time of the purest relation between Yahweh and Israel, while Ezekiel understands it as a time of Israel's utter rebellion and as a prefigurement of the final eschatological judgment. The examples of such contradictory views could be multiplied almost endlessly.

The amazing fact, however, is that the final editors of the canon included all of these opposing views in our Bible. If the Priestly writers edited the Old Testament, they nevertheless did not exclude Trito-Isaiah, despite its virulent attack upon them. They honored Trito-Isaiah's views. They let them stand. They affirmed, "Yes, this too is the Word of God, and therefore it must be included along with his other words to us." In short, the Priestly editors found that these words of Trito-Isaiah, which so judged their cultic ways, also mediated to them the truth of God and sustained their life in relation to him. They therefore were willing to be corrected and judged by Trito-Isaiah for the sake of their relationship with God.

Whenever we read the Bible, we must approach it in the same manner. We may find much in the Bible, especially in the Old Testament, that we do not like. We may encounter many passages that level awful judgment upon us and upon our ways. We may find views in the Old Testament that we think are contradictory to the views of the New Testament. But all such discoveries should not thereby be discarded. Rather, we should emulate the Priestly writers and preserve all the traditions, keeping them and pondering them in our hearts. Across the centuries, the church has found in its experience that these words of God in our canon give a true revelation of God and sustain us in our relationship with him. For the sake of that relationship, we must be willing to listen to the total canon, for in that relationship alone can we have abundant and eternal life.

With regard to the second question raised above, we should have no illusions about the writers of the Bible. Like us, every single one of them was a sinful human being. There were no pure and undefiled authors of our Scriptures, writing divine words dictated from heaven and untouched by human folly. There were only communities in a people called Israel, which found itself visited by the living God—communities of faithful folk who heard God speaking to them, who saw God at work in their midst, and who passed their testimonies to that working and speaking on to the next generations, until finally the Word has come down to us in the form of our canon.

Moreover, the amazing thing about these faithful folk was that they never claimed to be sinless. Throughout the Old Testament, the people of Israel confess, "We have never lived up to our election; we have never been faithful to the God who called us into being," just as in the New Testament, the disciples of Jesus constantly are shown to misunderstand and finally to desert their Lord. But God chose such people as the mediators of his Word and as the recipients of his judging and saving Presence with them, just as today he still chooses us to carry his Good News into all the world. The Word of God comes into and is mediated through actual, everyday human life! That fact, which is so clear in the disputes of Trito-Isaiah, is the hope of the world. God deals with us where and how we are. Finally he becomes our flesh in Jesus Christ. It is with this world and its vicissitudes that the Holy One of Israel is passionately concerned. And despite all our sin and shortcomings, and despite those of the biblical writers, God's Word that he speaks through the Scriptures is nevertheless so powerful that it truly mediates his Presence and activity to all of us who open our hearts to it in faith.

Finally, has the Word of Trito-Isaiah come to pass? Does the Word of our God stand forever? When we affirm in faith that Jesus Christ is the Word made flesh, we confess that it has and does. God keeps his Word in surprising ways, according to the Bible. He gathers up all his words in the Old Testament and reinterprets and corrects and completes them in the Person of his Son. We have seen how so much of the teaching of Trito-Isaiah is reiterated in the teaching of our Lord, and surely he finally becomes that Suffering Servant whose role the Levitical-prophetic party of Third Isaiah saw itself fulfilling. But we must also be conscious of the fact that, according to the New Testament, Jesus Christ replaces the new temple on Zion. He becomes the cornerstone of the new elect congregation of God. He mediates to them the new covenant, and gives them the new covenant commands to replace the law of Deuteronomy. He breaks the bounds of Israel's exclusiveness and brings foreigners into his kingdom of priests. He becomes our Source of freedom and joy and abundant life, which no one can take away from us. And he is the foundation of our certain hope that God's kingdom will come on earth, even as it is in heaven. Because of Christ—because in him the Word of God triumphed over even death itself—we know that the Word of God will stand forever. Nothing can defeat his purpose, and if we trust him, nothing and no one can snatch us out of his loving hands. Therefore,

Let us greatly rejoice in the Lord,
　let us exult in our God;
　for he has clothed us with the garments of salvation.
　　　　　　Amen.

Bibliography

Ackroyd, Peter R. *Exile and Restoration*. Philadelphia: Westminster, 1968.

Bright, John. *A History of Israel*. Third Edition. Philadelphia: Westminster, 1981.

Cross, Frank Moore. "The Priestly Houses of Israel." *Canaanite Myth and Hebrew Epic*. Cambridge: Harvard, 1973.

Hanson, Paul D. *The Dawn of Apocalyptic: The Historical and Sociological Roots of Jewish Apocalyptic Eschatology*. Revised Edition. Philadelphia: Fortress, 1975, 1979.

Klein, Ralph W. *Israel in Exile: A Theological Interpretation*. Overtures to Biblical Theology. Philadelphia: Fortress, 1979.

Kraus, H.-J. "Die ausgebliebene Endtheophanie, Eine Studie zu Jes. 56-66," *ZAW* 78, 1966, 317-32.

McKenzie, John L., S.J. *Second Isaiah*. The Anchor Bible. Garden City, N.Y.: Doubleday, 1968.

Muilenburg, James. "Exegesis of The Book of Isaiah." *The Interpreter's Bible*, Vol. V. Nashville: Abingdon, 1956.

Skinner, J. *The Book of the Prophet Isaiah*, Chs. XL-LXVI. Cambridge: at the University Press, 1910.

Smith, George Adam. *The Book of Isaiah*, Chs. XL-LXVI, Vol. II. Revised Edition. New York and London: Harper, n.d.

Westermann, Claus. *Isaiah 40-66: A Commentary*. The Old Testament Library. Translated by D. M. G. Stalker from the 1966 German edition. Philadelphia: Westminster, 1969.

Zimmerli, W. "Zur Sprache Tritojesajas," 1950, reprinted in *Gottes Offenbarung: Festschrift für L. Kohler*. Munich, 1963, 217-33.